Greater Bay Area Golf Guide

3rd Edition

INCLUDES THE ORIGINAL COUNTIES OF:

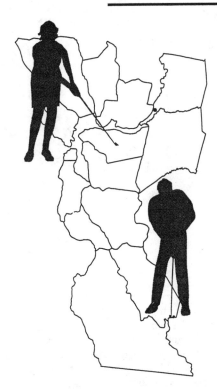

ALAMEDA
CONTRA COSTA
MARIN
MONTEREY
NAPA
SAN BENITO
SAN FRANCISCO
SAN MATEO
SANTA CLARA
SANTA CRUZ
SOLANO
SONOMA

PLUS COVERAGE IN:

LAKE TAHOE
RENO
SACRAMENTO
SAN JOAQUIN

Published by:
Locations Plus...

Greater Bay Area Golf Guide
by:
H. Grout & S. Grout

All information contained in this publication was provided or derived from provided materials by the individual golf courses. Every attempt was made to verify all information at the time of printing and is believed, by the publishers, to be both accurate and complete. However, due to the rapidness of change, not all information can be guaranteed to be error free. When calling for reservations we suggest asking about the courses' present green fees to eliminate possible confusion. If you believe that an error or an omission exists, please contact the publishers at the following address.

LOCATIONS PLUS
11578 S. Apache Trail
Conifer, CO 80433

(303) 838-8833

CONTENTS

CONTENTS

CONTENTS

CONTENTS

CONTENTS

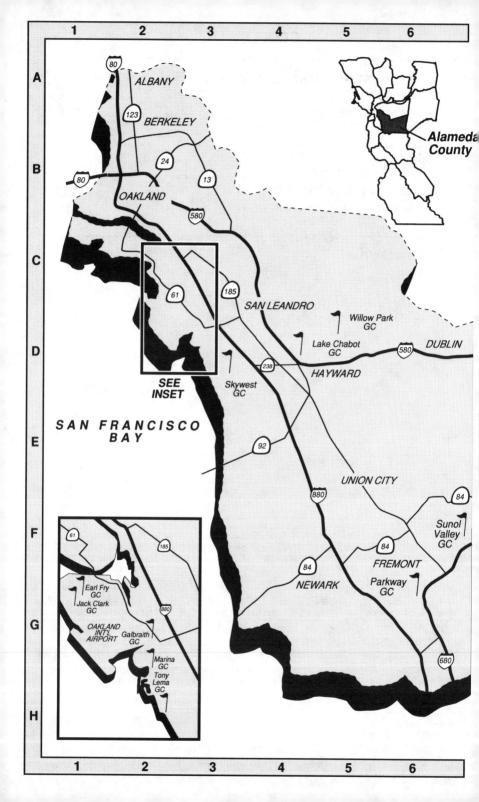

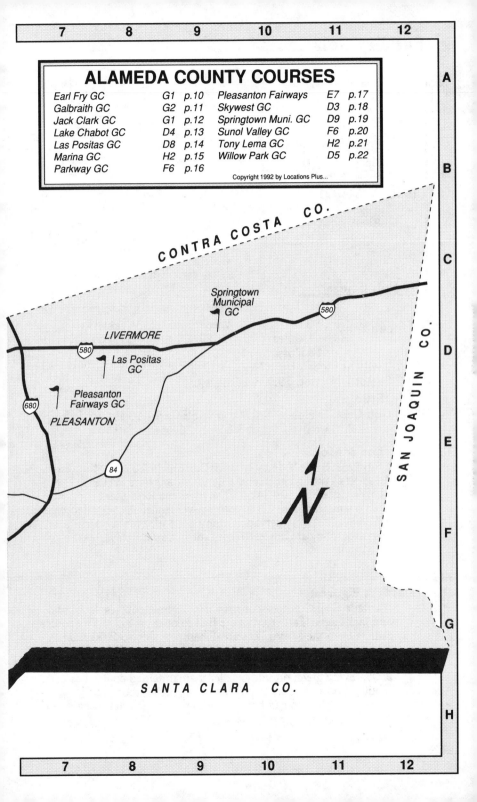

Earl Fry Golf Course

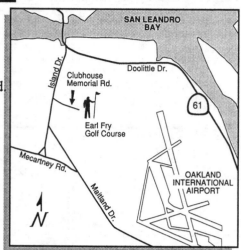

1 Clubhouse Memorial Rd.
Alameda, CA 94501

(510) 522-4321

18 Hole Course

Green Fees:

	Weekdays	Weekends
9 Holes:	$9.00	$11.00
18 Holes:	$14.00	$17.00

Twilight Rate: $8.00
Senior Discount: $9.00 weekdays only

Outfitting:

Golf Cars - 9 Holes: $10.00	Golf Cars - 18 Holes: $16.00
Pull Carts: $2.00	Clubs: $10.00

Lessons & More:

Club Pro: Steve Videtta   **Lessons:** $25 / 30 Minutes
A Practice Putting Green and a Driving Range are available.
Bucket prices: $1.50 - $4.50. The Alameda Restaurant is open
from 6 a.m. until 8 p.m. for your convenience. A cocktail lounge
is also available. Reservations can be made seven days in
advance. They are busiest Wednesdays thru Sundays, least busy
on Mondays.

Facts & Figures:

Alameda Golf Complex consists of 2, 18 hole courses, Earl Fry
and Jack Clark. Earl Fry was the first to open in 1927. The course
ratings from the Men's Tees are: Championship 69.2, Regular
67.6. Course ratings from the Women's Tees are: White 72.1,
Red 70.2. Par for the course is 71. Yardages range from 6141 to
5505. Every green on this excellently maintained course has been
rebuilt. It is a pleasure to play and challenging too. A ball
retriever might come in handy due to the many water hazards.

Galbraith Golf Course

10505 Doolittle Drive
Oakland, CA 94603

(510) 569-9411

18 Hole Course

Green Fees:

	Weekdays	Weekends
9 Holes:	n.a.	n.a.
18 Holes:	$11.00	$15.00
Twilight Rate: After 1 p.m.	$6.00	$9.00

Senior Discount: $8.00 on weekdays only.

Outfitting:

Golf Cars - 9 Holes:	Golf Cars - 18 Holes: $16.00
Pull Carts: $2.50	Clubs: $10.00

Lessons & More:

Club Pro: Dan Osterberg   **Lessons:** $25 / 30 Minutes
Galbraith Golf Course offers a Practice Putting Green, Chipping
Green and a Driving Range. Bucket prices: $1.50 - $7.00. Their
Snack Bar is open from 6 a.m. until 8 p.m. and a portable snack
bar has been added. The Pro Shop will help you in filling your
immediate golfing needs. Reservations can be made one week in
advance beginning at 6:00 a.m., Friday.

Facts & Figures:

This 18 hole championship course opened in 1967. It is a long
course measuring 6777 yards from the Blue Tees, 6298 yards
from the White Tees and 5732 yards from the Red Tees. Course
ratings are: 71.1, 69.9, and 71.7, respectively. Par for the course is
72. They have added a new man-made lake just right of a new
tee on the 18th hole. Overall the course is flat and is easy to
walk. There is a sufficient amount of trees and foliage to attract
many varieties of wildlife. This course is sometimes referred to as
being a refuge to some of the endangered species.

Jack Clark Golf Course

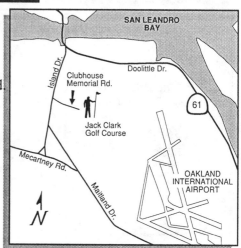

1 Clubhouse Memorial Rd.
Alameda, CA 94501

(510) 522-4321

18 Hole Course

Green Fees:

	Weekdays	Weekends
9 Holes:	$9.00	$11.00
18 Holes:	$14.00	$17.00

Twilight Rate: $8.00
Senior Discount: $9.00 weekdays only

Outfitting:

Golf Cars - 9 Holes: $10.00   Golf Cars - 18 Holes: $16.00
Pull Carts: $2.00   Clubs: $10.00

Lessons & More:

Club Pro: Steve Videtta   **Lessons:** $25 / 30 Minutes
A Practice Putting Green and a Driving Range are available.
Bucket prices: $1.50 - $4.50. The Alameda Restaurant is open
from 6 a.m. until 8 p.m. for your convenience. A cocktail lounge
is also available. Reservations can be made seven days in advance.

Facts & Figures:

Jack Clark was added to the Alameda Golf Complex in 1956.
This 18 hole course is rated 70.8 from the Championship Tees,
and 68.5 from the Regular Tees. Course ratings from the
Women's Tees are: White 73.0, Red 69.3. Par for the course is
71. Yardage for the course ranges from 6559 to 5473. This
course is a little longer than Earl Fry and substantially drier. If
you are not comfortable playing around water then Jack Clark
would be a better choice.

Lake Chabot Municipal Golf Course

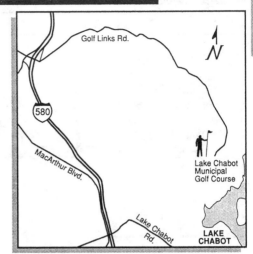

11450 Golf Links Rd.
Oakland, CA 94605

(510) 351-5812

18 Hole Course

Green Fees:

	Weekdays	Weekends
9 Holes:	n.a.	n.a.
18 Holes:	$11.00	$15.00

Twilight Rate: After 1 or 3 p.m. $6.00 $9.00
Senior Discount: $16.00 Monthly Ticket + Surcharge

Outfitting: (Rates for Golf Cars vary)

Golf Cars - 9 Holes: n.a.	Golf Cars - 18 Holes: $18.00
Pull Carts: n.a.	Clubs: $12.00

Lessons & More:

Club Pro: Jeffrey Dennis   Lessons: $30 / Lesson
Lake Chabot Golf Course has a Practice Putting Green and a
Driving Range sporting new distance signs and new mats.
Bucket prices: $2.00 - $3.00. Their Coffee Shop is open from
dawn to dusk. The Pro Shop handles a complete line of golf
equipment. Weekend reservations are taken on the prior Monday
beginning at 6:00 a.m. Weekday reservations can be made 7 days
in advance.

Facts & Figures:

Lake Chabot Golf Course has been in operation since 1923.
Total yardage from the Men's Tees is 6011 and 5278 from the
Women's Tees. The course is rated 67.3, and 68.6, respectively.
Par is 70/71. There is one par 6 hole, four par 5 holes, five par 3
holes, leaving the remaining 9 holes with a par of 4. The course
is very scenic and from the back side you can see the entire Bay
Area. This course hosts the Lake Chabot Pro-Am and the Oak-
land City Tournaments in September, and the Charles Peoples
Pro-Am in May.

13

Las Positas Golf Course

Clubhouse Drive
Livermore, CA 94551

(510) 443-3122

27 Hole Course

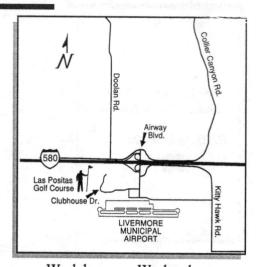

Green Fees:

	Weekdays	Weekends
9 Holes:	*$12.00	*$14.00
18 Holes:	$17.00	$25.00
Twilight Rate:	$10.00	$13.00

Senior Discount: Mondays only

Outfitting:

Golf Cars - 9 Holes: $10.00   Golf Cars - 18 Holes: $20.00
Pull Carts: $2.00   Clubs: $10.00/$15.00

Lessons & More:

Club Pro: Dan Lippstreu   **Lessons:** $25 / 30 Minutes
Las Positas offers a Practice Putting Green, Chipping Green and a
Driving Range having new mats. Bucket prices: $2.00 - $4.00. A
new Clubhouse is in the making. The Pro Shop will help fill your
immediate golfing needs. Weekend reservations can be made on
the prior Tuesday beginning at 7:00 a.m., for weekdays one week
in advance. Residents of Livermore receive a discount on Green
Fees. *9 Hole Executive Course Green Fees.

Facts & Figures:

This course has undergone a complete overhaul which was
completed in July of 1990. The course has been expanded to
include 27 holes. The Executive 9 is 2000 yards long with a Par
of 31. The 18 hole course is 6683 yards long from the Blue Tees
with a par of 72. The course provides plenty of shade trees if you
wander off the fairways. There are lakes and creeks presenting
water hazards throughout the course. The lack of hills makes it
easy to walk.

Marina Golf Course

13800 Neptune Drive
San Leandro, CA 94577

(510) 895-2164

9 Hole Course

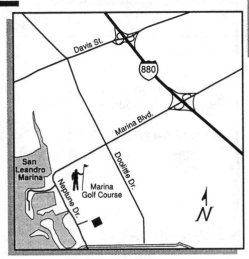

Green Fees:

	Weekdays	Weekends
9 Holes:	$6.00	$7.00
18 Holes:	$9.00	$10.00

Twilight Rate:
Senior Discount: Residents of San Leandro only.

Outfitting:

Golf Cars - 9 Holes:	$6.00	Golf Cars - 18 Holes:	$12.00
Pull Carts:	$3.00	Clubs:	$10.00

Lessons & More:

Club Pro: Steve Elbe   **Lessons:** $25 / 30 Minutes
This course is the 9 hole Executive course of the San Leandro
Golf Complex. They have a new lighted Practice area that
includes a Driving Range. Bucket prices: $1.25 - $4.00. The Brass
Putter Restaurant is open from dawn until 8 p.m. The Steve Elbe
Golf Shop carries a complete line of golf merchandise. Reserva-
tions can be made one week in advance beginning at 6:00 a.m.

Facts & Figures:

This course opened originally with 9 holes in 1963. A temporary
additional 9 was added in 1974 pending completion of the Tony
Lema championship 18 hole course. Marina reverted back to its'
original layout and is a nine hole course today. With only 1658
yards, par 29, distance is not a major factor when playing this
course, but accuracy is. Only two of the holes are par 4's and the
rest are par 3's. You might consider this a warm-up course before
starting out on Tony Lema's.

15

Parkway Golf Course

3400 Stevenson Blvd.
Fremont, CA 94538

(510) 656-6862

9 Hole Course

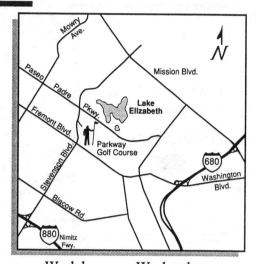

Green Fees:

	Weekdays	Weekends
9 Holes:	$5.50	$7.50
18 Holes:	$7.50	$11.00

Twilight Rate: n.a.
Senior Discount: $4.50 9 holes / $6.50 18 holes, weekdays only

Outfitting:

Golf Cars - 9 Holes: n.a.	Golf Cars - 18 Holes: n.a.
Pull Carts: $2.00	Clubs: $4.00

Lessons & More:

Club Pro: Mike Pope   Lessons: $20 / 30 Minutes
Parkway Golf Course offers a Practice Putting Green and a
Driving Cage. They have a Snack Bar and lounge for your
convenience. A Pro Shop will help in filling your immediate
golfing needs. Reservations can be made one week in advance
beginning at 7:00 a.m. Their busiest day of the week is Sunday,
least busy day is Monday.

Facts & Figures:

Parkway Golf Course originally opened in 1971 with 18 holes. It
has recently lost it's back 9 holes and is now a 9 hole, par 3
course. It is a true delight for the golfer who prefers to play nine
holes. Just because this is a par 3, don't assume it is an easy
course. You will find plenty of sandtraps and water hazards to
challenge your accuracy. Total yardage of the course is now
1024. It is rated 49.0 for the Men and 50.3 for the Women.
Slope rating: 67. Parkway hosts the Saturday Men's Championship, the Anniversary Tournament and Club Tournaments each
year.

Pleasanton Fairways Golf Course

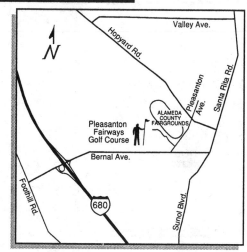

4501 Pleasanton Ave.
Pleasanton, CA 94566

(510) 462-4653

9 Hole Course

Green Fees:

	Weekdays	Weekends
9 Holes:	$7.00	$8.00
18 Holes:	$13.50	$15.50

Twilight Rate: n.a.
Senior Discount: $5.75 Wkdays. / $7.00 Wknds. for 9 Holes

Outfitting:

Golf Cars - 9 Holes: n.a.	Golf Cars - 18 Holes: n.a.
Pull Carts: $1.50	Clubs: $6.00

Lessons & More:

Club Pro: Steve Fluke   Lessons: $30 / Lesson
Pleasanton Fairways offers a Practice Putting Green, Chipping Green and a Driving Range. Bucket prices: $1.75 - $3.50. Only irons are allowed on this range. They have a newer regulation driving range across the road where Bill Corbett is the teaching professional. The Snack Bar is open daily serving a variety of refreshments. The Pro Shop is complete. Reservations are taken Monday thru Sunday.

Facts & Figures:

Construction on this nine hole course was completed in 1974. To add country charm, it is situated in the center of the oval race track in the Alameda Country Fairgrounds. As you might guess, it is a fairly short course measuring 1,755 yards. Par for the course is 29 and the course record is 25 which indicates it is not an easy course. There are three par 4 holes, and the rest are par 3's. Course rating is 54.4.

17

Skywest Golf Course

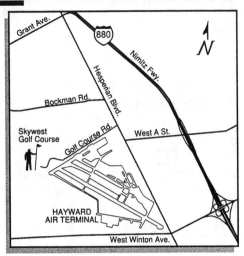

1401 Golf Course Road
Hayward, CA 94541

(510) 278-6188

18 Hole Course

Green Fees:

	Weekdays	Weekends
9 Holes:	$8.00	*$10.00
18 Holes:	$12.00	$15.00

Twilight Rate: *$10 - 9 holes after 3 on wknds. or 1st 2 hrs of day
Senior Discount: Monthly tickets for residents only

Outfitting:

Golf Cars - 9 Holes: $10 / $11   Golf Cars - 18 Holes: $17 / $18
Pull Carts: $3.00   Clubs: n.a.

Lessons & More:

Club Pro: Cheryl Pastore   Lessons: $35 / 30 Minutes
Skywest Golf Course provides a Practice Putting Green and a
Driving Range that has just been upgraded. Bucket prices: $2.50 -
$3.50. The Skywest Restaurant is open daily from sunrise to
sunset. The Pro Shop carries a complete line of golf accessories.
Reservations can be made seven days in advance, Sat. for Sat.,
etc., beginning at 6:00 a.m. Their busiest day is Friday, least
busy on Thursday.

Facts & Figures:

This 18 hole course opened in 1965. Major renovations have
already been completed, the last being the planting of an additional 250 trees. This course is long, the fairways are defined by
rough and the greens are large. The course is in excellent condition. From the Blue Tees it is 6930 yards long, rated 72.8/121.
From the White Tees it is 6540 yards long, rated 70.9/116.
Women's yardage is 6171, rated 74.3/123.   Par for the course is
72/73. Course records are 65 from both sets of Men's Tees and a
68 from the Ladies' Tees. Skywest regularly hosts the Hayward
City Championship Tournament during February.

Springtown Municipal Golf Course

939 Larkspur Drive
Livermore, CA 94550

(510) 455-5695

9 Hole Course

Green Fees:

	Weekdays	Weekends
9 Holes:	$10.00	$12.00
18 Holes:	$15.00	$18.00

Twilight Rate: n.a.
Senior Discount: Monthly pass: $55 single, $70 couple.

Outfitting:

Golf Cars - 9 Holes: $10.00   Golf Cars - 18 Holes: $20.00
    Pull Carts: $2.00   Clubs: $5.00

Lessons & More:

Club Pro: Mike Orlando   **Lessons:** $20 / 45 Minutes
Springtown Municipal offers a Practice Putting Green, Chipping
area and a Driving Cage. The price of a bucket of balls is $2.00.
The Springtown Coffee Shop serves a full breakfast and lunch,
plus an assortment of beverages, including beer and wine. Their
Pro Shop carries a complete line of golf accessories. Reservations
can be made at any time. Their least busy day of the week is
Tuesday.

Facts & Figures:

This 9 hole course opened approximately 28 years ago. It has a
separate set of tees for playing a second nine. The course measures 5710 yards long from the Men's Tees and 5332 yards from
the Women's Tees. Par for the course is 70. The course is rated
65.4 from the Men's White and Blue Tees, and 69.5 from the
Women's Red and White Tees. The course is well varied with
doglegs, water hazards and sandtraps. The excellent undulating
greens can offer some very difficult pin placements. The fairways
are open, but you still have the possibility of hitting a tree now
and then.

19

Sunol Valley Golf Course

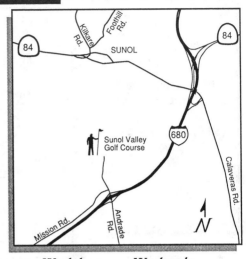

6900 Mission Road
Sunol, CA 94586

(510) 862-0414

36 Hole Course

Green Fees:

	Weekdays	Weekends
9 Holes:	n.a.	n.a.
18 Holes:	$18.00	*$40.00
Twilight Rate: After 2:00	$14.00	$15.00

Senior Discount: Monthly purchase

Outfitting: *Golf Car included in weekend Green Fee
Golf Cars - 9 Holes: n.a.   Golf Cars - 18 Holes: $24.00
    Pull Carts: n.a.   Clubs: $20.00

Lessons & More:

Club Pro: Jerry Thormann   Lessons: $25 / Lesson
Sunol Valley has two 18 hole golf courses, The Palms and
The Cypress. They have a Practice Putting Green and
Chipping Green, but no Driving Range. Their cafe is open
from 6 a.m. until 5 p.m., a cocktail lounge is also available.
Reservations can be made seven days in advance beginning at
6:30 a.m., Sat. for Sat., etc. A Golf Car is mandatory on
weekends.

Facts & Figures:

The Sunol Valley Golf Course is set in the scenic valley of
Mission Hills. The Palms Course is the longest of the two
courses measuring 6843 yards from the Blue Tees, 6409 yards
from the White Tees and 5997 from the Red Tees. You will find
the fairways are generous and more forgiving then those of the
Cypress Course. The Cypress measures 6195 yards from the
Blue Tees, 5801 yards from the White Tees, and 5458 yards from
the Women's Tees. Par 72 applies to both courses.

Tony Lema Golf Course

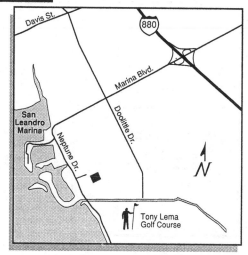

13800 Neptune Drive
San Leandro, CA 94577

(510) 895-2162

18 Hole Course

Green Fees:

		Weekdays	Weekends
9 Holes:		n.a.	n.a.
18 Holes:		$12.00	$16.00
Twilight Rate:	2:00 p.m.	$9.00	$11.00

Senior Discount: San Leandro residents-weekdays only

Outfitting:

Golf Cars - 9 Holes:	Golf Cars - 18 Holes: $16.00
Pull Carts: $3.00	Clubs: $10.00

Lessons & More:

Club Pro: Steve Elbe   **Lessons:** $25 / 30 Minutes
This 18 hole course is part of the San Leandro Golf Complex.
They have a new complete practice area that is lighted along with
a Driving Range. Bucket prices: $1.50 - $4.50. The Brass Putter
Restaurant is open from dawn until 8 p.m., a cocktail lounge is
also available. The Steve Elbe Golf Shop carries a complete line
of golf merchandise. Reservations can be made one week in
advance starting at 6:00 a.m. Residents of San Leandro receive a
discount on Green Fees.

Facts & Figures:

This championship 18 hole course was completed in 1983. It is
sitting on the eastern edge of the San Francisco Bay, across from
the yacht harbor and an assortment of fine restaurants. Total
yardage from the Championship Tees is 6636, rating is 69.2;
yardage from the Regular Tees is 6175, rating is 67.1. Women's
total yardage is 5718, rating is 71.3, slope is 108. Par for the
course is 72. Tony Lema Golf Course regularly hosts the Coor's
sponsored People's Pro-Am Tournament.

Willow Park Golf Course

17007 Redwood Road
Castro Valley, CA 94546

(510) 537-8989

18 Hole Course

Map showing Lake Chabot, Willow Park Golf Course, Lake Chabot Rd., Fairmont Dr., Seven Hills Rd., Redwood Rd., N

Green Fees:

	Weekdays	Weekends
9 Holes:	$10.00	$12.00
18 Holes:	$14.00	$18.00

Twilight Rate: n.a.
Senior Discount: n.a.

Outfitting:

Golf Cars - 9 Holes: $12.00   Golf Cars - 18 Holes: $22.00
Pull Carts: $2.00   Clubs: n.a.

Lessons & More:

Club Pro: Bob Bruce   **Lessons:** $16 / 30 Minutes
Willow Park Golf Course offers a Practice Putting Green and a
Driving Range. Bucket prices: $1.00 - $3.00. Their restaurant is
open from 10 a.m. until 10 p.m., Tuesday through Sunday. A
cocktail lounge is also available. A complete line of golf accessories can be found at the Pro Shop. Weekend reservations can be
made on the Monday prior in early a.m., weekday reservations
are taken ten days in advance.

Facts & Figures:

This Par 71, eighteen hole golf course opened in January of 1967.
The course record of 63 has not been beaten since 1968. Yardage
from the Championship Tees is 6227, from the Men's regular
Tees it is 5465 and it is 5200 from the Women's Tees. There is a
lovely creek making its way through this course, which, as you
might guess, often comes into play. There is enough variation in
the landscape at Willow Park to keep most golfers interested.

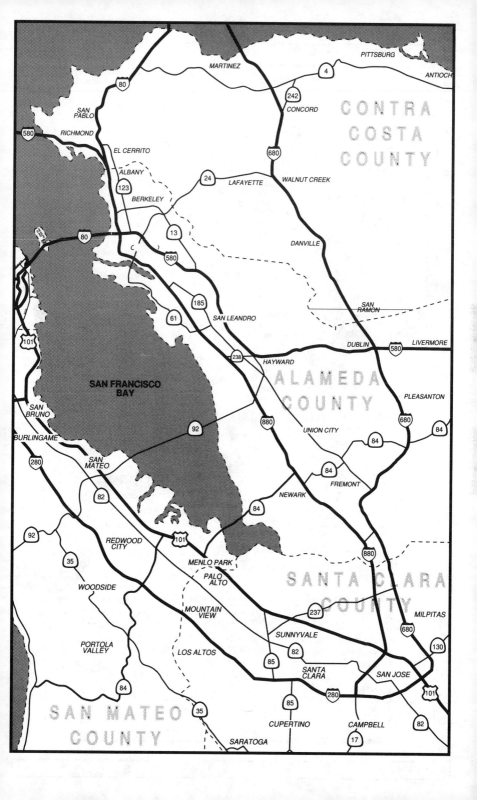

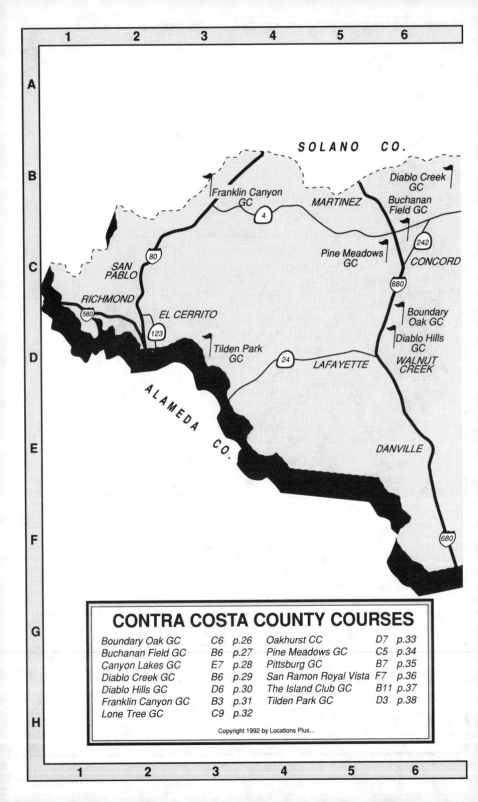

CONTRA COSTA COUNTY COURSES

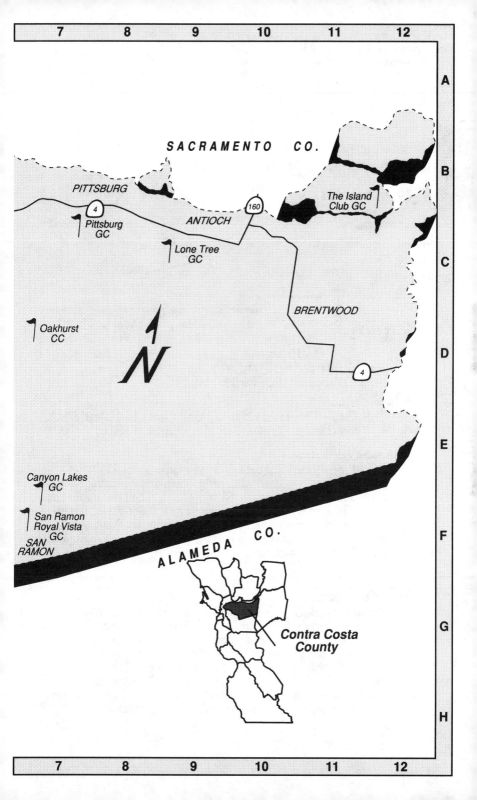

Boundary Oak Golf Course

3800 Valley Vista Road
Walnut Creek, CA 94598

(510) 934-6211

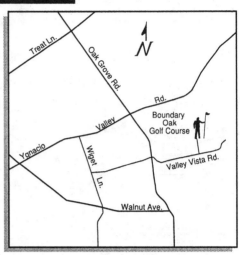

18 Hole Course

Green Fees:

	Weekdays	Weekends
9 Holes:	$9.00	$12.00
18 Holes:	$13.00	$17.00

Twilight Rate: After 2:00 p.m. $7.00
Senior Discount: With weekly play cards

Outfitting:

Golf Cars - 9 Holes: $12.00	Golf Cars - 18 Holes: $20.00
Pull Carts: $3.00	Clubs: $10.00

Lessons & More:

Club Pro: Robert T. Boldt   Lessons: 6 for $150
A Practice Putting Green, Chipping Green and a Driving Range
are available. Bucket prices: $3.00 - $5.00. Their restaurant and
lounge is open from dawn to dusk. The Pro Shop is complete.
Weekday reservations can be made by phone on Sundays starting
at 9:00 a.m. and for weekends starting at 1:00 p.m. Walnut Creek
residents receive a discount on Green Fees.

Facts & Figures:

Boundary Oak Golf Course is nicely situated on a hillside. It is a
pleasant course without any fairway bunkers to contend with and
only a minimal amount of water hazards. From the Championship Tees it is 6788 yards long, rated 72.0. From the Regular Tees
it is 6406 yards long, rated 70.2. The Women's yardage is 5705,
rated 72. Slope 117. Par for the course is 72. Craig Elliott holds
the course record with a 65 from the Championship Tees. In mid
July Boundary Oak hosts the Contra Costa Amateur.

Buchanan Field Golf Course

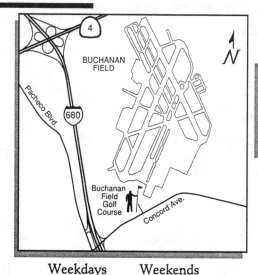

3330 Concord Avenue
Concord, CA 94520

(510) 682-1846

9 Hole Course

Green Fees:

	Weekdays	Weekends
9 Holes:	$8.50	$10.00
18 Holes:	$12.50	$15.00

Twilight Rate: n.a.
Senior Discount: Weekdays - $7 for 9 holes - $55 for 10 plays

Outfitting:

Golf Cars - 9 Holes: $9.00   Golf Cars - 18 Holes: 18.00
Pull Carts: $2.00   Clubs: $5.00

Lessons & More:

Club Pro: Tim Sullivan   Lessons: $30 / 30 Minutes
Buchanan Field Golf Course offers a Practice Putting Green and a
Driving Range. Bucket prices: $4.00 - $5.00. The Back-9
Restaurant is open from 7 a.m. until 5 p.m. for your convenience.
The Pro Shop carries a full line of golf equipment. Reservations
can be made one week in advance. Their busiest day is Saturday,
least busy day is Monday.

Facts & Figures:

This public nine hole course opened in 1961. Since then they
have planted 400 trees to encourage more accuracy in the golfer's
shots. This is a challenging nine holes, it plays for a total of 2616
yards. Par for the Men is 33, Women's par is 36. The course
rating for 18 holes is 63.0 for the Men, and 64.0 for the Women.
The course is fairly flat and is ideal for the beginner golfer.

Canyon Lakes Country Club

640 Bollinger Canyon Wy.
San Ramon, CA 94583

(510) 735-6511

18 Hole Course

Green Fees:

	Weekdays	Weekends
9 Holes:	$29.00	*$32.00
18 Holes:	$50.00	*$60.00

Twilight Rate: n.a.
Senior Discount: n.a.   *Fees apply Friday, Sat. & Sun.

Outfitting:
Golf Cars included in Green Fees
Golf Cars - 9 Holes: **Golf Cars - 18 Holes:**
Pull Carts: n.a.   Clubs: $15.00

Lessons & More:
Club Pro: Russ Dicks   Lessons: $30 / 30 Minutes
Canyon Lakes is open every day except Monday. A Practice
Putting Green is the only warm-up practice facility offered. They
have a new clubhouse and a complete Pro Shop. Reservations
can be made seven days in advance. Their busiest days are
Fridays thru Sundays, least busy day is Tuesday. Use of a golf
car is mandatory; it is included in the Green Fee.

Facts & Figures:
This 18 hole golf course, open since 1987, is located in the rolling
hills of San Ramon. The course name, Canyon Lakes, properly
describes the scenic landscape. Yardage from the Championship
Tees is 6379 and from the Men's Tees it is 5975. It is rated 70.1
and 68.2, respectively. From the Women's Tees it is 5234 yards
long and is rated 69.3. Par for the course is 71, the course record
stands at 65.

Diablo Creek Golf Course

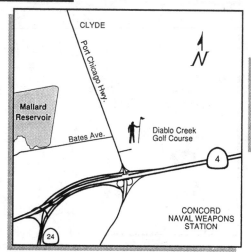

4050 Port Chicago Hwy.
Concord, CA 94520

(510) 686-6262

18 Hole Course

Green Fees:

	Weekdays	Weekends
9 Holes:	*$9.50	*$12.50
18 Holes:	$15.50	$18.50

Twilight Rate: Same as 9 Hole Fees.
Senior Discount: Residents only.

Outfitting:

Golf Cars - 9 Holes: $9.00   Golf Cars - 18 Holes: $16.00
         Pull Carts: $3.00   Clubs: $10.00

Lessons & More:

Club Pro: **Lessons:** $25 / 30 Minutes
Diablo Creek Golf Course offers a Practice Putting Green and a
Driving Range. Bucket prices: $2.00 - $3.75. Their full restaurant
and sprots bar is open daily from 6 a.m. until 10 p.m. Their Pro
Shop is complete. Reduced Green Fees available to Concord
residents and they may make weekend reservations on the prior
Saturday. Non-residents may reserve tee times on the prior
Monday. ***9 Hole rates available before 7:30 a.m.**

Facts & Figures:

Diablo Creek Golf Course originally opened as a 9 hole course in
1962. In 1972 an additional 9 holes were added. The course
plays for a total of 6763 yards from the Blue Tees, 6344 from the
White Tees and 6000 from the Red. From the White Tees it is
rated 69.3 with a slope of 107. They have been busy shaping up
this beautiful 18 hole course.

Diablo Hills Golf Course

1551 Marchbanks Drive
Walnut Creek, CA 94598

(510) 939-7372

9 Hole Course

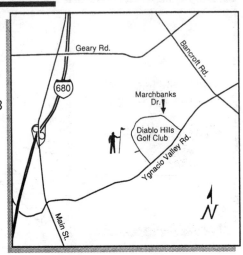

Green Fees:

	Weekdays	Weekends
9 Holes:	$10.00	$13.00
18 Holes:	$14.00	$25.00

Twilight Rate: n.a.
Senior Discount: $9.00 / 9 holes weekdays only; Jrs. $5.50

Outfitting:

Golf Cars - 9 Holes: $12.00   Golf Cars - 18 Holes: $24.00
Pull Carts: $2.00   Clubs: $5.00

Lessons & More:

Club Pro: Nick Andrakin   Lessons: $30 / 30 Minutes
Diablo Hills Golf Course offers a Practice Putting Green, Chipping Green but no Driving Range. The Greenery Restaurant is open from 7 a.m. to 10 p.m. daily, a lounge is also available. Their Pro Shop will help fill your immediate golfing needs. Weekend reservations can be made anytime and they take weekday reservations one month in advance. Their busiest day is Sunday, least busy on Thursday.

Facts & Figures:

This 9 hole course opened in 1975. It winds its way through a picturesque setting of condominiums. When playing this course you need to bring your sandwedge for it is heavily sprinkled with sandtraps, but you can leave your ball retriever at home because you won't find any water. Men's yardage from the Blue Tees is 2302, and from the Women's Red Tees it is 2173. Par for the course is 34. Diablo Hills regularly hosts the Singh's Invitational Golf Tournament.

Franklin Canyon Golf Course

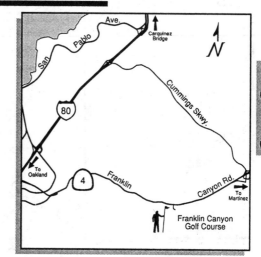

California Highway 4
Rodeo, CA 94572

(510) 799-6191

18 Hole Course

Green Fees:

	Weekdays	Weekends
9 Holes:	n.a.	n.a.
18 Holes:	$18.00	$30.00
Twilight Rate:	$9.00	$13.00
Senior Discount: n.a.		

Outfitting:

Golf Cars - 9 Holes: Golf Cars - 18 Holes: $22.00
   Pull Carts: $3.00   Clubs: $15.00

Lessons & More:

Club Pro: Brett Smithers   Lessons: $25 / Lesson
This golf course offers a Practice Putting Green, Chipping Green and a Driving Range sporting new mats and range balls. Bucket prices: $2.00 - $4.00. Their Snack Bar is open from dawn until 5 p.m. daily, a cocktail lounge is also available. The Pro Shop carries a complete line of golf accessories. Weekend reservations can be made seven days in advance beginning at 6:00 a.m. Busiest day is Saturday, least busy day is Tuesday.

Facts & Figures:

This 18 hole course, designed by Robert Muir Graves, opened in March of 1968. The Clubhouse and Pro Shop were added in 1970. From the Championship Tees it plays for 6776 yards and is rated 70.9. From the Regular Men's Tees it is 6202 yards long and is rated 68.9. Yardage from the Women's Tees is 5516 and is rated 71.2. Overall par for the course is 72. The course record stands at 63. Franklin Canyon annually hosts the Northern California Firefighters Open, the Northern CA Seniors Open and the West County Tournament. This is a fairly long and difficult course for any experienced level of golfer.

31

Lone Tree Golf Course

4800 Lone Tree Way
Antioch, CA 95431

(510) 757-5200

18 Hole Course

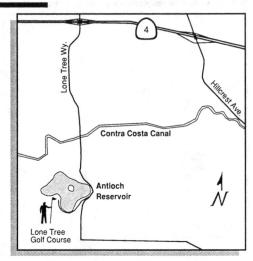

Green Fees:

	Weekdays	Weekends
9 Holes:	$8.00	n.a.
18 Holes:	$9.50	$12.00

Twilight Rate: $8.00 after 3:00
Senior Discount: n.a.

Outfitting:

Golf Cars - 9 Holes: $10.00	Golf Cars - 18 Holes: $16.00
Pull Carts: $3.00	Clubs: $7.50

Lessons & More:

Club Pro: Pat Cain   Lessons: $20 / 30 Minutes
Lone Tree Golf Course offers a Practice Putting Green and a
Driving Range. Bucket prices: $2.00 - $4.00. Their Snack Bar is
open from dawn to dusk. A cocktail lounge is also available. The
Pro Shop carries a complete line of golf equipment. Weekend
reservations can be made on the Saturday prior and seven days in
advance for weekdays.

Facts & Figures:

Lone Tree is an eighteen hole, championship course. It falls in
the middle between difficult and easy. It is a pleasant course
having a fair amount of hills and trees. They have recently
reconstructed 3 of their greens. From the Championship Blue
Tees the total yardage is 6387, from the Regular White Tees it is
6073 and from the Women's Red Tees it is 5769. Course ratings
and slopes are: 69.8/116, 67.8/112 and 71.8/100, respectively.
Overall par for the course is 72.

32

Oakhurst Country Club

8000 Clayton Road
Clayton, CA 94517

(510) 672-9737

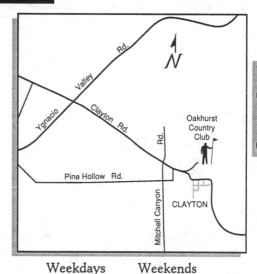

18 Hole Course

Green Fees:

	Weekdays	Weekends
9 Holes:	n.a.	n.a.
18 Holes:	$50.00	$70.00
Twilight Rate:	$39.00	$45.00
Senior Discount:	n.a.	

Outfitting:

Golf Cars - 9 Holes: Golf Cars - 18 Holes: Included
Pull Carts: n.a. Clubs: $25.00

Lessons & More:

Club Pro: Dennis Simon Lessons: $30 / 30 Minutes
This new facility offers a Practice Putting Green, Chipping Green and a Driving Range. Bucket prices: $3.00 - $5.00. They have a complete Snack Bar that is open each morning one-half hour before the first Tee-Time. Their Pro Shop carries a complete inventory of golf equipment. Reservations may be made three days in advance. Golf Cars are mandatory, they are included in the Green Fees.

Facts & Figures:

This new, semi-private, challenging course, opened in October of 1990. It is located at the base of Mt. Diablo which accounts for the hilly terrain. The greens are undulating and fast. You can count sixty bunkers through this 18 hole course and water hazards on several of the holes. From the Championship Tees the course is a whopping 6937 yards long with a slope of 132. Slope from the Ladies' Tees is 123.

Pine Meadow Public Course

451 Vine Hill Way
Martinez, CA 94553

(510) 288-2881

9 Hole Course

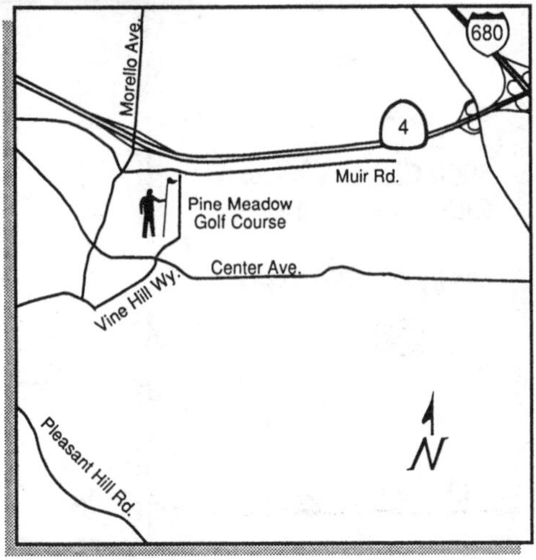

Green Fees:

	Weekdays	Weekends
9 Holes:	$6.00	$8.00
18 Holes:	$10.00	$14.00
Twilight Rate: n.a.		
Senior Discount:	$5.00	$8.00

Outfitting:

Golf Cars - 9 Holes: $8.00   Golf Cars - 18 Holes: $16.00
          Pull Carts: $2.00   Clubs: $4.00

Lessons & More:

Club Pro: **Lessons:** n.a.
A Practice Putting Green is available here at Pine Meadow, but no
Chipping Green or Driving Range. A Pro Shop will assist you in
filling your immediate golfing needs. A cocktail lounge is also
available. Reservations can be made at anytime.

Facts & Figures:

Pine Meadow Golf Course opened in 1966. This 9 hole, par 3
course sits on approximately 32 acres of land located in residential Martinez. It is a well maintained, straight, tree lined course
measuring 1360 yards. The holes range in length from 90 yards
on the 7th hole to 200 yards on the 9th. Men's par is 27,
Women's is 30. The course record stands at 25. The tees and
small greens are elevated adding difficulty and demanding
accurate approach shots. The very gentle rolling hills makes
walking pleasurable.

Pittsburg G & CC (Delta View GC)

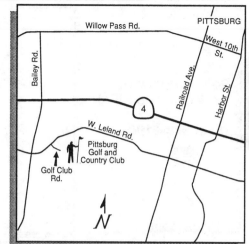

2222 Golf Club Road
Pittsburg, CA 94565

(510) 427-4940

18 Hole Course

Green Fees:

	Weekdays	Weekends
9 Holes:	$9.50	$11.50
18 Holes:	$11.50	$13.50

Twilight Rate: $6.00 for 9 Holes
Senior Discount: n.a.

Outfitting:

Golf Cars - 9 Holes: $9.00	Golf Cars - 18 Holes: $15.00
Pull Carts: $3.00	Clubs: $10.00

Lessons & More:

Club Pro: Jeff Fernandez   Lessons: $30 / 30 Minutes
A Practice Putting Green, Chipping Green and lighted Driving
Range, having new grass tees, are available at Delta View Golf
Course. A 30 ball Bucket: $1.50. The Restaurant is open from 11
a.m. until 3 p.m. Mon. thru Sun. Reservations are taken on
Saturday, beginning at 6:00 a.m. for the following Monday
through Sunday.

Facts & Figures:

With the completion of the new 9 holes in 1991, Pittsburg Golf
and Country Club is now a full 18 hole course. The original 9
holes have been renovated making the entire course a good test
for the low handicap player. Yardage from the Men's Tees is
6359, rated 70.4, slope 124. From the Women's Tees it is 5405
yards long, rated 70.4 with a slope of 118. The course has
recently changed their name to Delta View Golf Course.

San Ramon Royal Vista Golf Club

9430 Fircrest Lane
San Ramon, CA 94583

(510) 828-6100

$\nearrow$ N

18 Hole Course

Green Fees:

	Weekdays	Weekends
9 Holes:	*$11.00	*$15.00
18 Holes:	$17.00	$27.00

Twilight Rate: Same as 9 Hole Rates
Senior Discount: Monthly tickets good Monday - Friday.

Outfitting:

Golf Cars - 9 Holes: $12.00   Golf Cars - 18 Holes: $18.00
Pull Carts: $3.00   Clubs: $12.00

Lessons & More:

Club Pro: Patty Largent   Lessons: $30 / 60 Minutes
A Practice Putting Green, Chipping Green and a Driving Range
are available at San Ramon Royal Vista Golf Course. Bucket
prices: $2.50 - $4.00. Their restaurant is open from dawn until
dark, a cocktail lounge is also available. The Pro Shop carries a
complete line of golf equipment. Reservations can be made
seven days in advance beginning at day break. *9 Hole rates
available after 1:00 p.m.

Facts & Figures:

This championship 18 hole course first opened under the name of
San Ramon National. Located in the valley, the gentle rolling
hills and tree lined fairways help make a day of golf an outdoor
pleasure. Yardage from the Championship Tees is 6558, and
6319 from the Men's. It is rated 70.5 and 69.3, respectively.
Yardage from the Women's Tees is 5793 and is rated 71.4.

The Island Club Golf Course

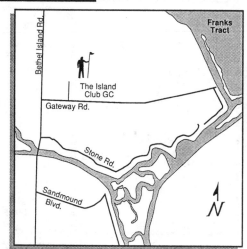

3303 Gateway Road
Bethel Island, CA 94511

(510) 684-2654

18 Hole Course

Green Fees:

	Weekdays	Weekends
9 Holes:	$8.50	n.a.
18 Holes:	$11.00	$15.00
Twilight Rate: At 4:00 p.m.	$7.00	$12.00

Senior Discount: $7 / 9 Holes & $9 / 18 Holes weekdays only

Outfitting:

Golf Cars - 9 Holes: $11.00   Golf Cars - 18 Holes: $18.00
Pull Carts: $3.00   Clubs: $7.50

Lessons & More:

Club Pro: Lessons: $20 / 30 Minutes
A Practice Putting Green, Chipping Green and Driving Range are available at The Island Club Golf Course. The cost of a bucket of practice balls is $2.00. Their restaurant is open from 7 a.m. until 2 p.m., the lounge remains open until 8 p.m. The Pro Shop carries a full line of golf equipment. Reservations can be made seven days in advance. Check with the Pro Shop for other Green Fee Specials.

Facts & Figures:

This Championship, eighteen hole golf course, previously known as Bethel Island, is relatively straight except for a few doglegs, the most severe is located on the 8th hole. Total playing yards from the Championship Tees is 6333, rating is 69.4. Yardage from the Regular Tees is 6120 and is rated 68.8. From the Women's Tees it is 5713 yards long and rated 71.3. Men's par is 72, Women's par is 74. Slope ratings from the Blue and White Tees is 114 and from the Red 113. This course is in good shape.

Tilden Park Golf Course

Grizzly Peak Blvd.
& Shasta Road
Alameda, CA 94708

(510) 848-7373

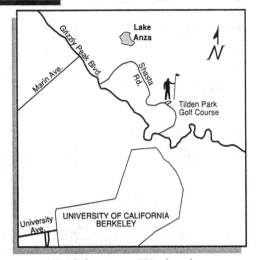

18 Hole Course

Green Fees:

	Weekdays	Weekends
9 Holes:	$10.00	$14.00
18 Holes:	$15.00	$20.00
Twilight Rate:	$10.00	

Senior Discount: With membership offer.

Outfitting:

Golf Cars - 9 Holes:	Golf Cars - 18 Holes: $22.00
Pull Carts: $4.00	Clubs: $12.00

Lessons & More:

Club Pro: Paul Wyrybkowski **Lessons:** Available
Tilden Park Golf Course offers a Practice Putting Green and a
Driving Range. Bucket prices: $1.75 - $6.00. Their Snack Bar is
open from 6:30 a.m. until 6:00 p.m. The Pro Shop is fully
stocked. Reservations can be made seven days in advance
beginning at 6:30 a.m. Their busiest days are Thursdays and
Fridays, least busy Mondays and Tuesdays.

Facts & Figures:

Tilden Park opened in 1935. For the last twenty years it has been
managed by the American Golf Corporation. This is a championship 18 hole course. Total yards from the Championship Tees is
6294; 5823 from the Men's Tees and from the Women's it is 5399
yards long. Ratings are: 69.9, 67.8 and 69.7, respectively. Overall par for the course is 70. Tilden Park annually hosts the Bay
Regionals. This is a very hilly course, so don't look for too many
flat lies. This course is beautiful, well secluded and offers a
challenge to all levels of golfers.

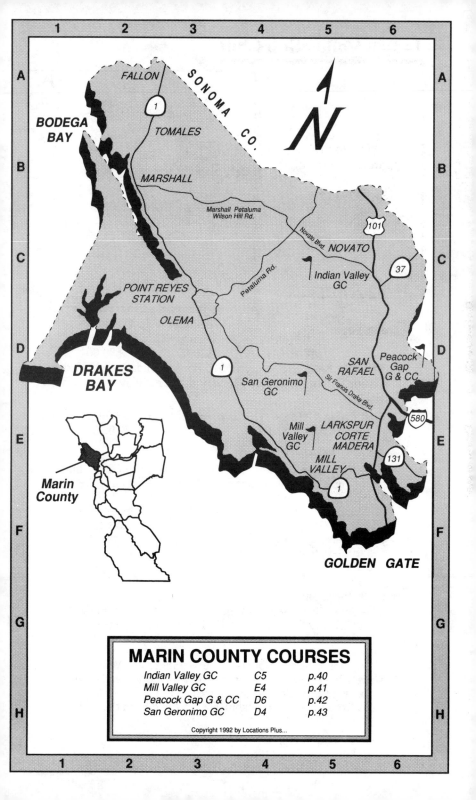

MARIN COUNTY COURSES

Indian Valley Golf Club

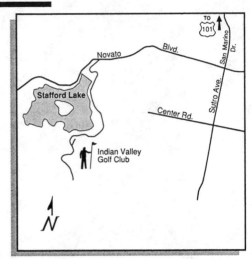

3035 Novato Blvd.
Novato, CA 94948

(415) 897-1118

18 Hole Course

Green Fees:

	Weekdays	Weekends
9 Holes:	n.a.	n.a.
18 Holes:	*$20.00	$30.00

Twilight Rate: $15 Wkdys. / $16 Fri. & Holidays / $25 Wknds.
Senior Discount: $15.00 Monday thru Thursday

Outfitting:

Golf Cars - 9 Holes: $13.00   Golf Cars - 18 Holes: $20.00
    Pull Carts: $3.00   Clubs: $10.00

Lessons & More:

Club Pro: Ron Hoyt   **Lessons:** $40 / 30 Minutes
This course offers a Practice Putting Green, Chipping Green and a
Driving Range. Cost of a large bucket is $4.00. Their restaurant
and lounge, "The 19th Hole", is open from 8 a.m. until 3 p.m.
The Pro Shop is complete. Reservations can be made seven days
in advance beginning at 7:00 a.m. Their busiest day of the week
is Saturday, their least busy day is Tuesday. ***Friday Green Fees
are $25.00.**

Facts & Figures:

This course is aptly named, Indian Valley, because it uniquely
winds its way through the valley making a complete circle. It is
heavily tree lined, with many rolling fairways. You will encounter water hazards on eleven of the holes, so having a ball retriever
along would be appropriate. Course ratings are: Women's 70.7,
slope 128, Men's Championship 69.2, slope 119 and Regular
67.3, slope 116. Par for the course is 72. Yardages range from
6272 from the Championship Tees to 5304 from the Red Tees.

Mill Valley Golf Course

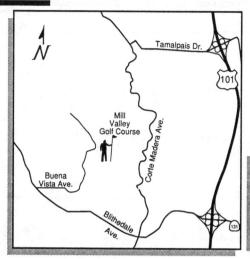

280 Buena Vista Ave.
Mill Valley, CA 94941

(415) 388-9982

9 Hole Course

Green Fees:

	Weekdays	Weekends
9 Holes:	$7.00	$10.00
18 Holes:	$9.00	$12.00
Twilight Rates:	$5.00	$6.00

Senior Discount: $5 / 9 holes, $7 / 18 holes

Outfitting:

Golf Cars - 9 Holes: $8.00   Golf Cars - 18 Holes: $14.00
Pull Carts: $1.50   Clubs: $5.00

Lessons & More:

Club Pro: Steve Yuhas   **Lessons:** n.a.
Mill Valley Golf Course offers a Practice Putting Green as their warm-up facility. They have a Snack Bar open daily and a small Pro Shop. Reservations accepted for Tee Times starting before 9:00 a.m., then it is on a first come, first served basis. Golf spikes are required for all golfers.

Facts & Figures:

This beautiful old 9 hole course opened in 1919. It is quite picturesque with the older forestry and a creek that flows through the course presenting water hazards on 6 of the holes. The hilly terrain does not often allow for flat lies. The course plays for a total of 4215 yards from the Men's Tees, is rated 60.6, slope 100. From the Ladies' Tees it is 4154 yards long and is rated 63.7. Par is 65/67. There are no par 5 holes.

41

Peacock Gap Golf & Country Club

Marin County

333 Biscayne Drive
San Rafael, CA 94901

(415) 453-4940

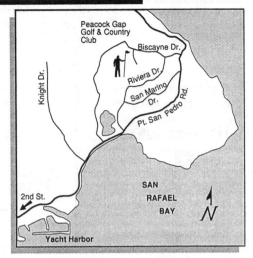

18 Hole Course

Green Fees:

	Weekdays	Weekends
9 Holes:	n.a.	n.a.
18 Holes:	$25.00	$30.00
Twilight Rate:	$18.00	$23.00
Senior Discount:	n.a.	

Outfitting:

Golf Cars - 9 Holes: $10.00   Golf Cars - 18 Holes: $20.00
Pull Carts: $3.00   Clubs: $18.00

Lessons & More:

Club Pro: Al Hand *   **Lessons:** $40 / 30 Minutes
A Practice Putting Green, Chipping Green and Driving Range are
available at Peacock Gap Golf and Country Club. Bucket prices:
$2.00 - $4.00. Their full restaurant is open 10 - 3 on weekdays, 7
- 3 on weekends. Their Pro Shop is complete. *Al Hand is the
Teaching Pro. Weekend reservations can be made on the Thursday prior at 12 noon, weekday reservations can be made seven
days in advance.

Facts & Figures:

This semi-private golf course has a par of 71 for the Men, and 72
for the Women. Course ratings from the Men's Tees, Championship: 69.7, slope 121, Regular: 67.9, slope 118. Ratings from the
Women's Tees, Red: 71.4, slope 114, White: 73.3 - slope 120.
This is not a terribly long course, yardage from the Championship Tees is 6284, but don't mistake that to mean that the course
is easy, even for the experienced golfer.

San Geronimo Golf Course

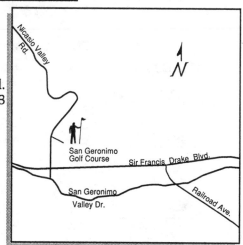

5800 Sir Francis Drake Bl.
San Geronimo, CA 94963

(415) 488-4030

18 Hole Course

Green Fees:

	Weekdays	Weekends
9 Holes:	*$20.00	$25.00
18 Holes:	*$35.00	$45.00

Twilight Rates: Same as 9 Hole Fees
Senior Discount: Club seniors: $15.00 on weekends

Outfitting:

Golf Cars - 9 Holes:	Golf Cars - 18 Holes: $20.00
Pull Carts: n.a.	Clubs: $15.00

Lessons & More:

Club Pro: Doug Talley   Lessons: $30 / Lesson
The San Geronimo Golf Course offers a Practice Putting Green
and a Chipping Green, but no Driving Range. For your convenience, San Geronimo has a snack bar, full restaurant and lounge.
Their Pro Shop carries a complete line of golf accessories. Reservations can be made one week in advance. *Friday Green Fees
are $22.00 for 9 Holes and $40 for 18 Holes.

Facts & Figures:

This Championship golf course re-opened in October, 1988 after
being refurbished by architect Robert Muir Graves. It is now a
semi-private course and reservations are needed. This course,
located 20 miles north of San Francisco, surrounded by various
parks, is in a picturesque valley setting. This par 72 course is
rated: Blue 71.9, White 70.6, and Red 73.4. This is a fairly long
course, 6669 yards from the Championship Tees, 6338 from the
White Tees, and 5865 from the Ladies' Tees. San Geronimo will
permit you a pleasurable game of golf away from the crowds.

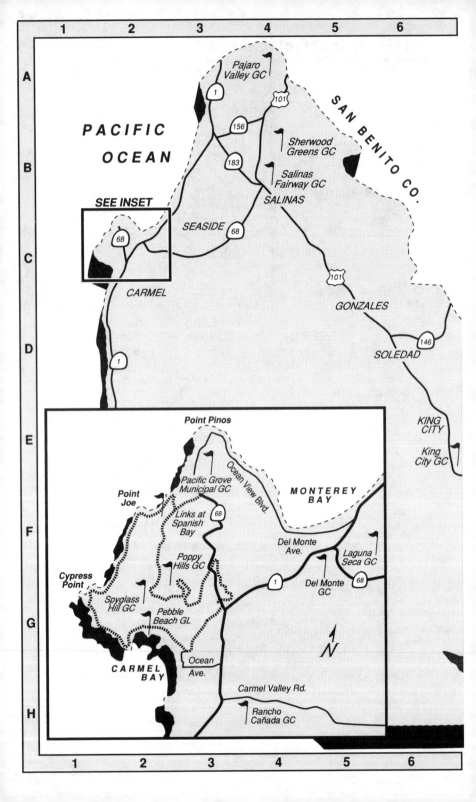

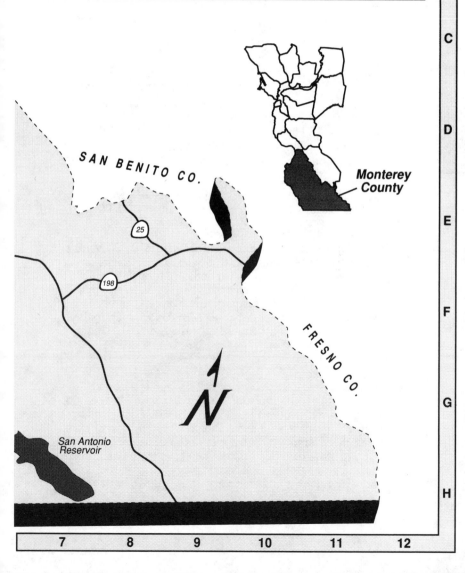

MONTEREY COUNTY COURSES

Del Monte GC	G5	p.46	Poppy Hills GC	F2	p.52
King City GC	E6	p.47	Rancho Cañada GC	H4	p.53
Laguna Seca GC	F5	p.48	Salinas Fairway GC	B4	p.54
Pacific Grove Muni. GC	E3	p.49	Sherwood Greens GC	B4	p.55
Pajaro Valley GC	A4	p.50	Spyglass Hill GC	G2	p.56
Pebble Beach GL	G2	p.51	The Links-Spanish Bay	F3	p.57

SAN BENITO CO.

25

198

FRESNO CO.

Monterey County

San Antonio Reservoir

Del Monte Golf Course

1300 Sylvan Road
Monterey, CA 93940

(408) 373-2436

18 Hole Course

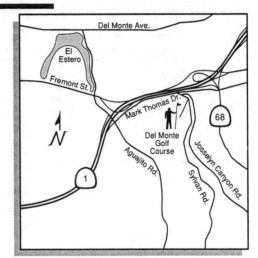

Green Fees:

	Weekdays	Weekends
9 Holes:	n.a.	n.a.
18 Holes:	*$40.00	*$45.00

Twilight Rate: $10.00, non-resident $15.00
Senior Discount: $20. 7-11 a.m. Mon. & Wed. cart included

Outfitting:

Golf Cars - 9 Holes: Golf Cars - 18 Holes: $22.00
     Pull Carts: $5.00   Clubs: $25.00

Lessons & More:

Club Pro: Joe Holdridge   **Lessons:** $20 / 30 Minutes
There is a Practice Putting Green but no Driving Range or Chipping Green. The Del Monte Bar and Grill is open from 7:30 a.m. to 2:30 p.m. for your convenience. The Pro Shop carries a complete line of golf accessories. Reservations can be made 60 days in advance. *Weekday rates Monday thru Thursday, Weekend rates, Friday, Saturday and Sunday.

Facts & Figures:

Del Monte Golf Course opened in 1897 and it is believed to be the oldest golf course west of the Mississippi still in operation on its original soil. This is a long, and overall, a relatively flat course, but by no means a beginners. Due to a combination of small greens, many sandtraps and a great deal of forestry your golfing skills will often be called upon. They have recently completed rebuilding four greens. Del Monte plays host to the ESPN Jr. World Tournament and also some NFL Tournaments.

King City Golf Course

613 So. Vanderhurst Ave.
King City, CA 93930

(408) 385-4546

9 Hole Course

Green Fees:

	Weekdays	Weekends
9 Holes:	$8.00	$9.00
18 Holes:	$12.00	$14.00

Twilight Rate: $5.00 / 9 Holes, $8.00 / 18 Holes, after 2:00 p.m.
Senior Discount: $6.00 / 9 Holes, $9.00 / 18 Holes, wkdys. only

Outfitting:

Golf Cars - 9 Holes: $8.00	Golf Cars - 18 Holes: $14.00
Pull Carts: $1.00	Clubs: $2.00

Lessons & More:

Club Pro: Jon Olson   Lessons: $15 / Lesson
King City Golf Course offers a Practice Putting Green, Chipping
Green and a Driving Range. Bucket prices: $1.25 - $2.50. Their
Snack Bar is open to serve you from 7 a.m. until 7 p.m. Their Pro
Shop is complete. Weekend reservations can be made on the
Monday prior beginning at 7:30 a.m., weekday reservations are
not necessary. Their busiest day is Friday, the least busy day is
Monday.

Facts & Figures:

King City Golf Course opened in 1953. Since that time, several
modifications have been made to the original layout. The course
is 5634 yards long from the White Tees and is rated 66.4
Women's rating is 70.3, yardage is 5350. Course par is 70, the
record is 62. This is a short, but challenging course. The King
City Junior Golf Tournament has been held here annually since
1957. King City has recently installed a new irrigation system,
and improved drainage.

Laguna Seca Golf Club

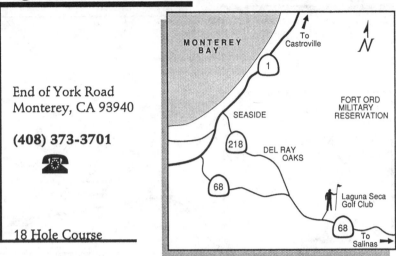

End of York Road
Monterey, CA 93940

(408) 373-3701

18 Hole Course

Green Fees:

	Weekdays	Weekends
9 Holes:	n.a.	n.a.
18 Holes:	$45.00	$45.00

Twilight Rate: $22.00 after 2:00 p.m./3:00 p.m.
Senior Discount: Tuesdays only with purchase of play card

Outfitting:

Golf Cars - 9 Holes:	Golf Cars - 18 Holes: $23.00
Pull Carts: $3.00	Clubs: $15.00

Lessons & More:

Club Pro: Dian Murphy   Lessons: n.a.
Laguna Seca Golf Club offers a Practice Putting Green and a Chipping Green but no Driving Range. Their new Clubhouse, restaurant and Pro Shop can more than fill your needs. Weekend reservations can be made one week in advance, Sat. for Sat., etc. They begin taking weekday reservations on the last Friday of the month for the following month.

Facts & Figures:

Laguna Seca Golf Club, designed by Robert Trent Jones, opened in 1970. Since it is located in the hills of the Monterey Peninsula, which has one of the finest climates, the course is referred to as "The Sunshine Course". This course offers you all the variety a championship course should, for instance, plenty of sand, trees, water, hills, and beauty. The course is rated 70.4 from the Championship Tees, 68.5 from the Men's, Par 71, and 70.2 from the Women's Tees, Par 72. You will find this course a pleasure to play.

48

Pacific Grove Municipal Golf Course

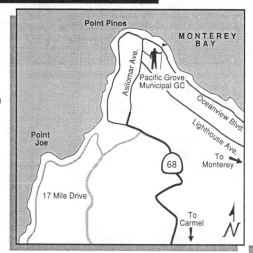

77 Asilomar Avenue
Pacific Grove, CA 93950

(408) 648-3177

18 Hole Course

Green Fees:

	Weekdays	Weekends
9 Holes:	$11.00	$14.00
18 Holes:	$17.00	$20.00

Twilight Rate: $10.00 after 3:00 p.m.
Senior Discount: n.a.

Outfitting:

Golf Cars - 9 Holes: $11.00   Golf Cars - 18 Holes: $20.00
Pull Carts: $2.50   Clubs: $20.00

Lessons & More:

Club Pro: Peter Vitarisi   **Lessons:** $25 / 30 Minutes
Pacific Grove Municipal offers a Practice Putting Green and a
Driving Range. Bucket price: $2.00. Their Snack Bar is open
from 7 a.m. to 4:30 p.m. for your convenience along with a Pro
Shop which carries a complete line of golf equipment. Weekend
reservations can be made 7 days in advance, Sat. for Sat., etc.,
beginning at 6:30., weekday reservations can be made 7 days in
advance at 6:50 a.m.

Facts & Figures:

Pacific Grove Municipal Golf Course originally opened in 1932 as
a 9 hole course, but in 1960 it was expanded to 18 holes. This
lovely old course sits on the tip of scenic Monterey Peninsula,
which is reason enough to ensure an enjoyable golf outing. A
beautiful old lighthouse, which sits in the middle of the course,
decorates the landscape. The length of the course from the
Men's Tees is 5553 yards, par 70, while from the Women's Tees
it is 5524 yards with a par of 72. Make sure to carry along a light
jacket in case you encounter some cool winds off the ocean.

Pajaro Valley Golf Club

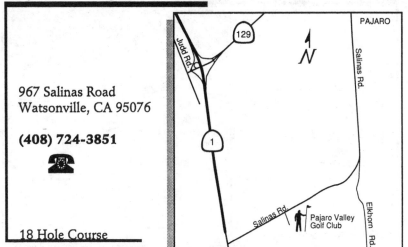

967 Salinas Road
Watsonville, CA 95076

(408) 724-3851

18 Hole Course

Green Fees:

	Weekdays	Weekends
9 Holes:	n.a.	n.a.
18 Holes:	$34.00	$45.00
Twilight Rate:	$22.00	$22.00
Senior Discount: n.a.		

Outfitting:

Golf Cars - 9 Holes: n.a.   Golf Cars - 18 Holes: $23.00
            Pull Carts: $3.00   Clubs: $12.00

Lessons & More:

Club Pro: Nick Lombardo   **Lessons:** $25 / 60 Minutes
There is a Practice Putting Green and a Driving Range available at
Pajaro Valley Golf Club. Bucket price: $3.00. Their Restaurant
and Bar is open from 7 a.m. until 4 p.m. Weekend reservations
can be made seven days in advance beginning at 6 a.m. Weekday
reservations can be made one month in advance beginning on the
Friday prior to the new month at 7 a.m. This course is busiest on
weekends, least busy on Mondays and Tuesdays.

Facts & Figures:

Pajaro Valley Golf Club opened in 1926 and reopened in 1990
after a fire. This well maintained golf course is challenging and
beautifully landscaped. The course is 6303 yards long from the
Men's Tees and 5642 yards from the Women's Tees. Course par
is 72. Ratings are, Men's 70.2 and Ladies' 71.0. Pajaro Valley
Golf Club regularly hosts the Little Helpers Golf Tournament.

Pebble Beach Golf Links

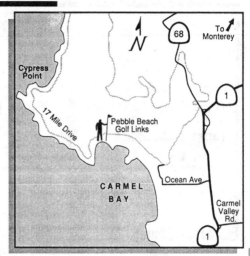

Seventeen Mile Drive
Pebble Beach, CA 93953

(408) 624-6611

18 Hole Course

Green Fees:

	Weekdays	Weekends
9 Holes:	n.a.	n.a.
18 Holes:	$200.00	$200.00

Twilight Rate: $75.00
Senior Discount: n.a.

Outfitting:

Golf Cars - 9 Holes: Golf Cars - 18 Holes: Included
Pull Carts: n.a.   Clubs: $35.00

Lessons & More:

Club Pro: R. J. Harper   Lessons: $40 / 30 Minutes
Pebble Beach offers a Practice Putting Green, Chipping Green and a Driving Range. The Gallery Restaurant offers a wide assortment of food and beverages, they are open from 6 a.m. to 4 p.m. daily. The Pro Shop carries a complete line of golf equipment. The Resort Lodge at Pebble Beach offer their guests a discount on Green Fees. Reservations can only be made one day in advance. Golf Cars are included in the Green Fees.

Facts & Figures:

Jack Neville and Douglas Grant designed this course that was dedicated in 1919. It is recognized as being one of the finest, most scenic golf courses in the world. It is the annual host to the AT&T Pebble Beach National Pro-Am. Total yardage from the Championship Tees is 6799, rating 75.0. From the White Tees it is 6357 yards long, rating 73.0 and 5195 from the Women's Tees, rating 70.3. Perennial ryegrass has been re-established on the fairways, restoration of all bunkers and rebuilding of greens #4, 5 and 7 to USGA specifications has just been completed.

51

Poppy Hills Golf Course

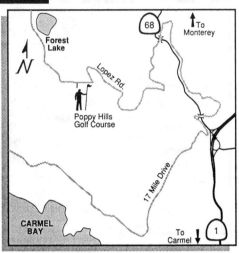

4501 Lopez Road
Pebble Beach, CA 93953

(408) 625-2035

18 Hole Course

Green Fees:

	Weekdays	Weekends
9 Holes:	n.a.	n.a.
18 Holes:	$85.00	$85.00

Twilight Rate: n.a.
Senior Discount: n.a.

Outfitting:

Golf Cars - 9 Holes: n.a.   Golf Cars - 18 Holes: $26.00
    Pull Carts: n.a.   Clubs: $25.00

Lessons & More:

Club Pro: John R. Geertsen   **Lessons:** $50 / 30 Minutes
Poppy Hills offers a Practice Chipping Green as well as a Driving
Range. Bucket prices: $2.00 - $4.00. For your convenience,
Poppy Hills Restaurant is open from 7 a.m. to 3 p.m. and their
Golf Shop carries a full line of merchandise. Reservations can be
made one month in advance on corresponding day. Their least
busy days of the week are Tuesdays through Thursdays.

Facts & Figures:

The Northern California Golf Association owns this golf course
which is operated by Poppy Hills, Inc. This course, designed by
Robert Trent Jones, II, opened on June 1, 1986. The setting, on
17 Mile Drive, will be enjoyed as you traverse this long, rolling
course. The course has 3 sets of Tees, the ratings for each are:
Blue - 74.6/slope 141, White - 71.7/slope 134, Red - 71.8/slope
128. The course record of 66 set in 1991 at the AT&T by Larry
Mize and John Cook. Most golfers will find this a most challenging course in a naturally beautiful setting.

Rancho Cañada Golf Club

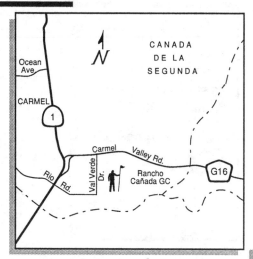

Carmel Valley Road
Carmel, CA 93922

(408) 624-0111

36 Hole Course

Green Fees:

	Weekdays	Weekends
9 Holes:	n.a.	n.a.
18 Holes:	$50.00	$50.00

Twilight Rate: $25.00 at 3 p.m. / $10.00 at 5 p.m.
Senior Discount: Yes

Outfitting:

Golf Cars - 9 Holes: n.a.	Golf Cars - 18 Holes: $23.00
Pull Carts: $3.00	Clubs: $25.00

Lessons & More:

Club Pro: Paul "Shim" La Goy **Lessons:** $35 / Lesson
Full practice facilities are available. They have a natural grass
Driving Range. Bucket prices: $3.00 - $4.00. Their Restaurant and lounge is open from 8 a.m. to 3 p.m. and weekends
from 6:30 a.m. until 3:00, closed Mondays. Their Golf Shop
is complete. Weekend reservations can be made one week in
advance beginning at 6:00 a.m. and 30 days in advance for
weekdays.

Facts & Figures:

At Rancho Cañada Golf Club you will find 2, exceptionally
beautiful and challenging, 18 hole championship courses. The
East opened first in 1970. This course lies at the foot of the Santa
Lucia Mountains and crosses back and forth over the Carmel
River. It measures 6434 yards long from the Championship Tees,
6034 from the White and 5255 yards from the Red. Ratings are
70.3, 68.7 and 69.0, respectively. The West Course is 6613 yards
long from the Blue, 6142 from the White and 5453 from the Red.
Ratings are 72.3, 69.5 and 70.5, respectively. The fairways are
narrow, straight shooting is a high priority.

Salinas Fairway Golf Course

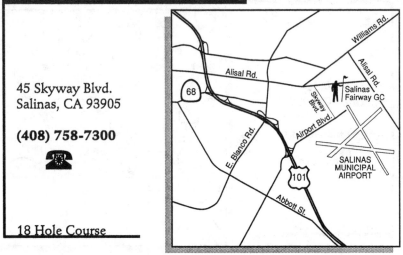

45 Skyway Blvd.
Salinas, CA 93905

(408) 758-7300

18 Hole Course

Green Fees:

	Weekdays	Weekends
9 Holes:	n.a.	n.a.
18 Holes:	$10.00	$12.50

Twilight Rate: $7.50 after 2:30 p.m.
Senior Discount: n.a.

Outfitting:

Golf Cars - 9 Holes: $8.00	Golf Cars - 18 Holes: $15.00
Pull Carts: $1.50	Clubs: $7.00 / $12.00

Lessons & More:

Club Pro: Kaiser / Stubblefield **Lessons:** $20.00 / Lesson
Salinas Fairway offers a Practice Putting Green, Chipping Green and a Driving Range. Bucket prices: $1.50 - $2.50. Their Snack Bar is open from dawn to dusk. The Pro Shop will help in filling your immediate golfing needs. Reservations for Saturdays can be made on Mondays prior and for Sundays, on Tuesdays prior. Weekday reservations are taken one week in advance.

Facts & Figures:

This 18 hole course is a highly regarded, well maintained municipal course. The slope rating of 111 will surprise the overconfident golfer. The course is relatively flat, with lateral as well as directly facing water hazards. Yardage from the Championship Tees is 6587, from the Men's Tees it is 6347 and from the Ladies' Tees it is 5674. Ratings are: 69.9, 68.8 and 70.8, respectively. The winds increase each afternoon so morning play is recommended.

Sherwood Greens Golf Course

1050 North Main Street
Salinas, CA 93906

(408) 758-7333

9 Hole Course

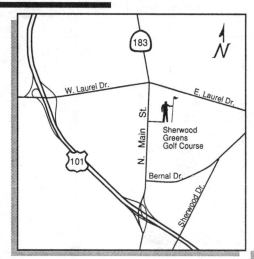

Green Fees:

	Weekdays	Weekends
9 Holes:	$4.75	$4.75
18 Holes:	$7.50	$7.50

Twilight Rate: n.a.
Senior Discount: n.a.

Outfitting:

Golf Cars - 9 Holes: n.a.   Golf Cars - 18 Holes: n.a.
Pull Carts: $1.00   Clubs: $2.50

Lessons & More:

Club Pro: Kaiser / Stubblefield   **Lessons:** $20 / 30 minutes
There is a Practice Putting Green, Chipping Green and a Driving
Range. Bucket prices: $1.75 - $3.00. Residents of Salinas receive
a discount on Green Fees. Reservations are not taken, first come,
first served.

Facts & Figures:

Right in the center of Salina's sporting area lies the Sherwood
Greens 9 hole golf course. The course is flat making it easy to
walk. The course ranks high with beginners and those looking
for a little practice with their irons. Except for one par 4 hole, all
the rest are par 3's. The shortest hole is 77 yards and the longest
is 251 yards. Total yardage is 1249, course par is 28. The rating
for 18 holes is 53.7 and the slope is 72.

Spyglass Hill Golf Course

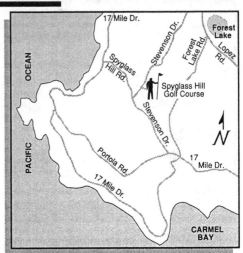

Spyglass Hill Road
& Stevenson Drive
Pebble Beach, CA 93953

(408) 624-3811

18 Hole Course

Green Fees:

	Weekdays	Weekends
9 Holes:	n.a.	n.a.
18 Holes:	$125.00	$125.00

Twilight Rate: $55.00
Senior Discount: n.a.

Outfitting:

Golf Cars - 9 Holes: Golf Cars - 18 Holes: Included
Pull Carts: n.a. Clubs: $35.00

Lessons & More:

Club Pro: Laird Small **Lessons:** $40 / 30 Minutes
A Practice Putting Green, Chipping Green and Driving Range are available. Bucket price: $3.00. The Pro Shop is completely equiped to help fill your golfing needs. The Spyglass Grill is open from dawn to dusk serving a wide variety of food and beverages. Reservations can be made 60 days in advance. Golf Car included in Green Fee.

Facts & Figures:

Spyglass Hill Golf Course was designed by Robert Trent Jones, Sr., and opened in 1966. This beautiful course is included in the AT&T Pebble Beach National Pro-Am and has been since 1967. The first official name was Pebble Beach Pines Golf Club. The name was changed to honor Robert Louis Stevensons' classic literary work *Treasure Island.* Each of the eighteen holes has a title taken from the novel. The first hole, appropriately named "Treasure Island", has a green completely surrounded by sand creating an island affect.

56

The Links at Spanish Bay

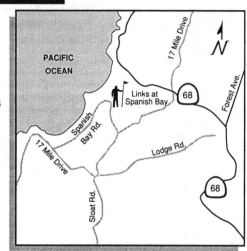

17 Mile Drive
Pebble Beach, CA 93953

(408) 624-6611

18 Hole Course

Monterey County

Green Fees:

	Weekdays	Weekends
9 Holes:	n.a.	n.a.
18 Holes:	$125.00	$125.00

Twilight Rate: $55.00
Senior Discount: n.a.

Outfitting:

Golf Cars - 9 Holes: Golf Cars - 18 Holes: Included
Pull Carts: n.a.   Clubs: $35.00

Lessons & More:

Club Pro: George Price   Lessons: *$30 / $40
A Practice Putting Green and a Chipping Green are available. The
Clubhouse Bar and Grill is open daily serving a varied assortment
of food and beverages. The Pro Shop carries a complete line of
golf accessories. Reservations can be made 60 days in advance.
* Lessons run for 30 minutes and vary in price from $30 with an
Assistant Pro to $40 for the Class "A" Pro. Golf Car included in
Green Fee.

Facts & Figures:

The course was designed by Tom Watson, Robert Trent Jones Jr.,
and Frank "Sandy" Tatum. This is a Scottish style link course,
characterized by rolling fairways and large expanses of sand
dunes. A large portion of the course is exposed to the prevailing
winds off the Pacific Ocean. The inland segment extends
through stands of Monterey pine in the Del Monte Forest,
offering a more sheltered environment. This championship
course measures 6820 yards from the Blue Tees, 6078 yards from
the White Tees, and 5287 yards from the Red Tees. Overall par is
72.

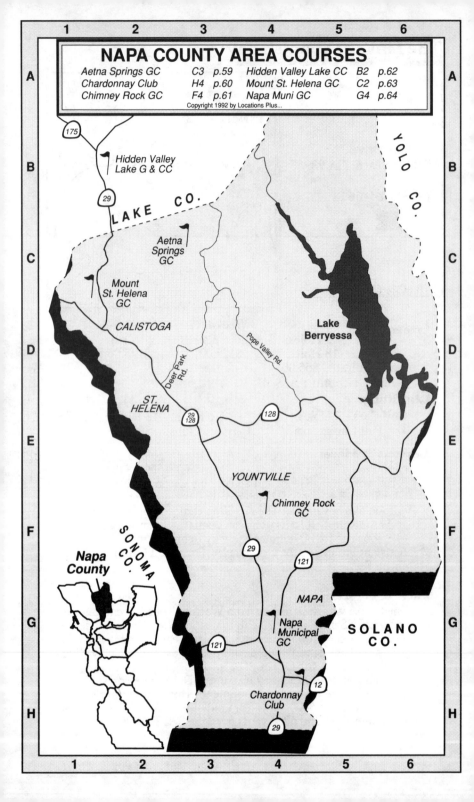

Aetna Springs Golf Course

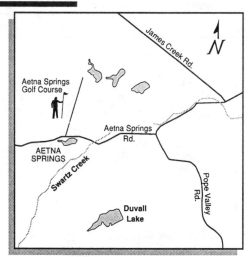

1600 Aetna Springs Rd.
Pope Valley, CA 94567

(707) 965-2115

9 Hole Course

Green Fees:

	Weekdays	Weekends
9 Holes:	$8.00	$10.00
18 Holes:	$8.00	$12.00
Twilight Rates:	$4.00	

Senior Discount: $5.00, weekdays only, age 60 plus

Outfitting:

Golf Cars - 9 Holes: $8.00	Golf Cars - 18 Holes: $15.00
Pull Carts: $1.00	Clubs: $5.00

Lessons & More:

Club Pro: Kent Stuth   Lessons: $35 / 60 Minutes
There is a new Driving Range and Putting green at Aetna Springs.
The Snack Shop is open from dawn to dusk. The Pro Shop is
complete. Reservations can be made one week in advance for
weekdays and weekends. Their busiest day of the week is
Sunday, least busy day is Tuesday.

Facts & Figures:

Aetna Springs Golf Course is one of the oldest courses in the
west. It opened in the late 1890's as part of the Aetna Springs
Resort. In the 1920's it was expanded to a full 9 holes and at that
time became a public course. Total yardage from the Men's Tees
is 2686 and 2527 from the Women's Tees. Par for 9 holes is 35.
Six of the holes are par 4's with 2 par 3's and 1 par 5. Course
rating is 64.7. The course has been upgraded to provide challenging play for both the beginner and the experienced player. The
sights are beautiful in the wooded Pope Valley setting.

Napa County

Chardonnay Club

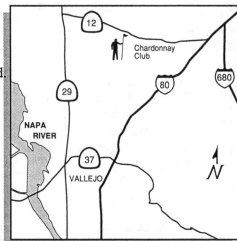

2555 Jameson Canyon Rd.
(California Highway 12)
Napa, CA 94558

(707) 257-8950

18 Hole Course

Green Fees:

	Weekdays	Weekends
9 Holes:	n.a.	n.a.
18 Holes:	$50.00	$60.00
Twilight Rates:	$35.00	$45.00
Senior Discount: n.a.		

Outfitting:

Golf Cars - 9 Holes:	Golf Cars - 18 Holes: Included
Pull Carts: n.a.	Clubs: $20.00

Lessons & More:

Club Pro: Mike Cook   **Lessons:** *Available
Promoting a "country club" atmosphere, all their warm-up facilities, even their driving range, are included in the Green Fees. Their grill serves breakfast and lunch. The Pro Shop carries a full line of golf accessories. *For more information on golf lessons, contact the Pro Shop. Reservations can be made one week in advance. Mandatory Golf Car included in Green Fees.

Facts & Figures:

Chardonnay Club has an 18 hole championship design set in the wine country of California. Yardage will range from 5000 to 6900. There are 5 separate teeing areas to accomodate every experience level of golfer. The landscape is varied to include wooded areas, ponds, streams, vineyards and the occasional open fairway that appeals to most golfers. A day at Chardonnay should prove to be most enjoyable.

Chimney Rock Golf Course

5320 Silverado Trail
Napa, CA 94558

(707) 255-3363

9 Hole Course

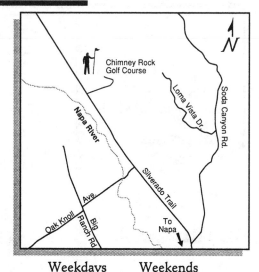

Green Fees:

	Weekdays	Weekends
9 Holes:	$12.00	$15.00
18 Holes:	$16.00	$20.00

Twilight Rates: Same as 9 hole fees.
Senior Discount: $7.50 Monday through Friday

Outfitting:

Golf Cars - 9 Holes:	Golf Cars - 18 Holes: $16.00
Pull Carts: $2.50	Clubs: $15.00

Lessons & More:

Club Pro: n.a.   **Lessons:** n.a.

A Practice Putting Green is available, but no Chipping Green or Driving Range. The Chimney Rock Coffee Shop is open from 6 a.m. until 9 p.m. for your convenience. The Pro Shop will help you in selecting merchandise to fill your golfing needs. Reservations can be made two weeks in advance. Reservations for more than 4 people requires a $5.00 deposit per person.

Facts & Figures:

This is a 9 hole championship golf course set in the beautiful wine country of Napa Valley. There is water directly in front of you as you tee off on two of the holes. The other hazards on the course are less threatening. You will find the greens here are fast and consistent and have been improved recently along with the rest of the course. Par for 9 holes is 36. Yardage from the Championship Tees is 3484, Men's yardage is 3386 and Women's' yardage is 2935. You will play two par 5 holes, two par 3 holes with the remainder being par 4's.

61

Hidden Valley Lake Golf & Country Club

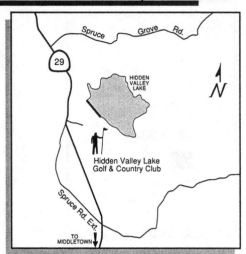

#1 Hartman Rd.
Middletown, CA 95461

(707) 987-3035

18 Hole Course

Green Fees:

	Weekdays	Weekends
9 Holes:	$10.00	$15.00
18 Holes:	$15.00	$24.00
Twilight Rates:	*$6.00	

Senior Discount: $8.00 on Wed., $3 off Mon.-Thur.

Outfitting:

Golf Cars - 9 Holes: $12.00   Golf Cars - 18 Holes: $18 / $20
Pull Carts: $2.00   Clubs: $8.00

Lessons & More:

Club Pro: Rob Kenny   Lessons: $20 / 30 Minutes
This course offers a Practice Putting Green and a Driving Range. A new Chipping Green is in the works. Their full restaurant and lounge is open from 7 a.m. until 5 p.m. daily. The Pro Shop offers a nice selection of golf equipment. Reservations can be made one week in advance. Their busiest day of the week is Saturday, least busy day is Thursday. *Special Golf Car rates available at Twilight.

Facts & Figures:

This 18 hole course was built in 1968 as part of the Boise-Cascade subdivision. The front 9 holes are flat and long. The back 9 holes are more picturesque as the course becomes hilly and additional trees line the fairways. You have an opportunity on 10 of the 18 holes to submerge your ball in a creek or pond crossing the fairways. The 15th hole offers a spectacular view of the valley from the 150 foot elevated tee area. Course yardages range from 6590 to 5593. Men's par is 72, Women's is 74. This course hosts the Hidden Valley Lake Pro-Am, and the Pacific Women's Golf Assoc. Team Championship.

Mount St. Helena Golf Course

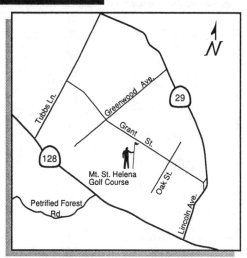

2025 Grant Street
Calistoga, CA 94515

(707) 942-9966

9 Hole Course

Green Fees:

	Weekdays	Weekends
9 Holes:	$10.00	$14.00
18 Holes:	$10.00	$14.00
Twilight Rates: After 4 p.m.	$5.00	$7.00

Senior Discount: $8.00 wkdys., $10:00 wknds. & holidays

Outfitting:

Golf Cars - 9 Holes: $8.00	Golf Cars - 18 Holes: $14.00
Pull Carts: $2.00	Clubs: $5.00

Lessons & More:

Club Pro: n.a.   Lessons: n.a.

This 9 hole course offers a Practice Putting Green, but no Chipping Green or Driving Range. The Snack Shop is open from dawn to dusk for your convenience. The Pro Shop will help fill your immediate golfing needs. They do not take reservations in advance, first come, first served.

Facts & Figures:

Mount St. Helena Golf Course is located in scenic Napa Valley. Overall par for the course is 68. Total yardage from the Men's Tees is 5420 and 5250 yards from the Women's Tees. There are only two par 3 holes on the course, the rest are par 4's. There are sufficient variations on this flat, easy to walk, course to hold the interest of most golfers. The abundant trees and narrow fairways test your golfing abilities.

Napa County

Napa Municipal Golf Course

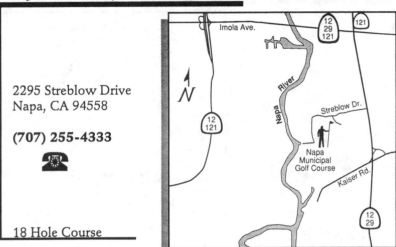

2295 Streblow Drive
Napa, CA 94558

(707) 255-4333

18 Hole Course

Green Fees:

	Weekdays	Weekends
9 Holes:	n.a.	n.a.
18 Holes:	$11.00	$17.00
Twilight Rates:	$7.00	$8.00

Senior Discount: Napa City residents only.

Outfitting:

Golf Cars - 9 Holes:	Golf Cars - 18 Holes: $17.00
Pull Carts: $3.00	Clubs: $15.00

Lessons & More:

Club Pro: Bob Swan   **Lessons:** $22.50 / 30 Minutes
Napa Municipal Golf Course offers a Practice Putting Green and a
Driving Range. Bucket prices: $1.50 - $3.00. The Out of Bounds
Restaurant is open daily for your convenience. The Pro Shop
carries a complete line of golf accessories. Reservations can be
made seven days in advance by phone beginning at 7:00 a.m.
This course is busiest on weekends, and least busy on Thursdays.

Facts & Figures:

This course opened in May of 1967. It is the qualifying site for
Kaiser, Anheuser-Busch Tour Tournaments. Total yardage from
the Blue Tees is 6730, from the White Tees it is 6506 and 5956
from the Red Tees. It is rated 71.7, 70.7 and 73.6, respectively.
Course par is 72/73. On 13 of the holes you will encounter a
water hazard either alongside or crossing the fairways. A number
of the doglegs are rather severe. This course is nick-named "JFK"
and "Kennedy" because of its location in the John F. Kennedy
Park.

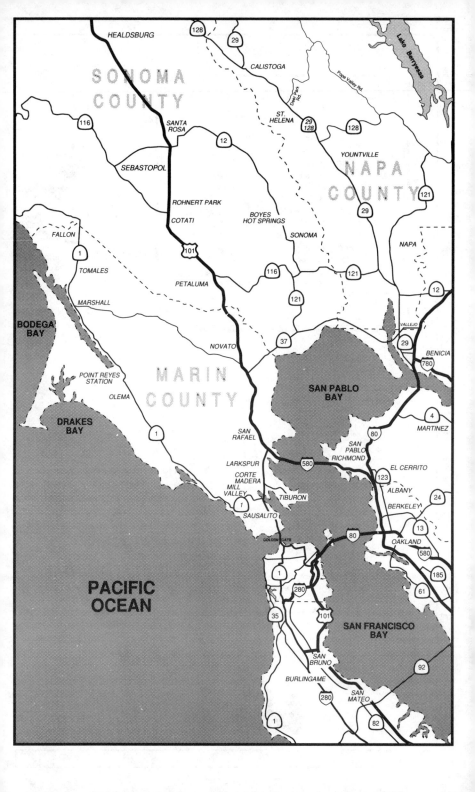

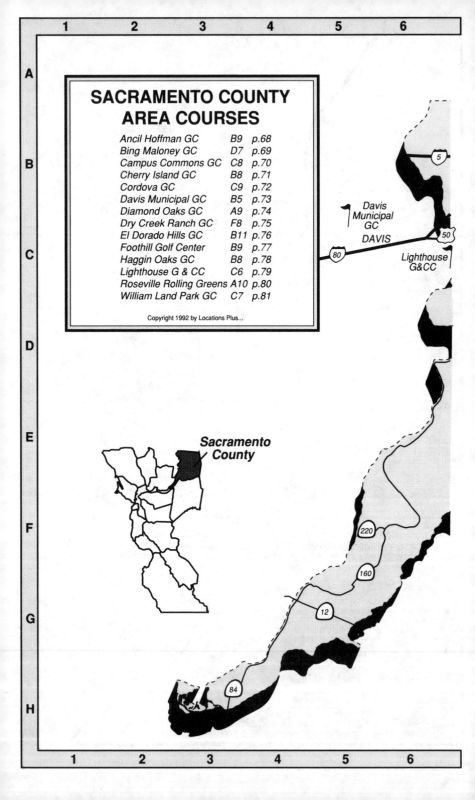

SACRAMENTO COUNTY
AREA COURSES

Davis
Municipal
GC

DAVIS

Lighthouse
G&CC

**Sacramento
County**

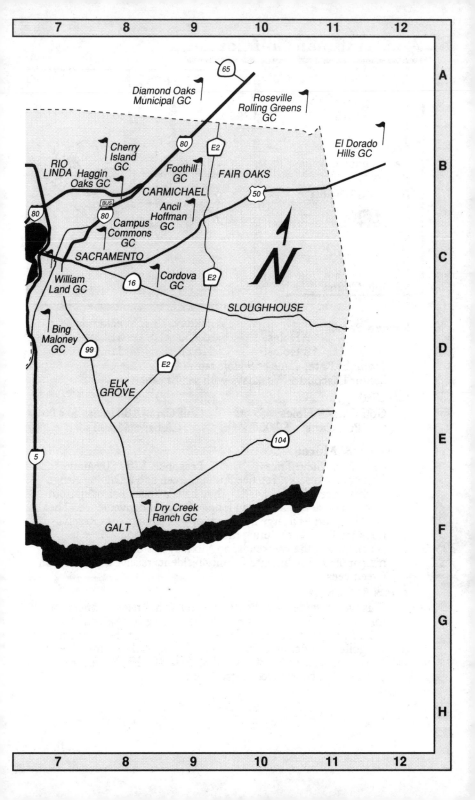

Ancil Hoffman Golf Course

6700 Tarshes Dr.
Carmichael, CA

(916) 482-5660

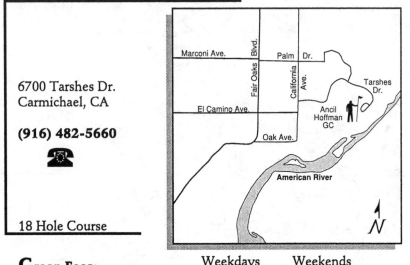

18 Hole Course

Green Fees:

	Weekdays	Weekends
9 Holes:	$9.50	$10.50
18 Holes:	$16.00	$18.00

Twilight Rate: Same as 9 Hole rates
Senior Discount: Weekdays with senior card

Outfitting:

Golf Cars- 9 Holes: $9.00   Golf Cars - 18 Holes: $18.00
    Pull Carts: $2.00   Clubs: $10.00

Lessons & More:

Club Pro: Steve Price   Lessons: $25 / 30 Minutes
This course offers a Practice Putting Green and a Driving Range. Bucket prices: $2.00 - $4.00. They have a Snack Bar open from dawn to dusk and a cocktail lounge for your convenience. The Pro Shop carries a large inventory of golf equipment. Reservations for Tee Times during the week can be made 7 days in advance. For the weekends, on Monday morings prior, beginning at 6:30. Sacramento County residents receive a discount on Green Fees.

Facts & Figures:

This well regarded, public 18 hole course has been in operation for the past 25 years. It is truly a challenging course with contoured greens and plenty of trees that will cause great difficulty to the golfer wandering off the narrow fairways. From the Blue Tees total yardage is 6800, rated 71.9, slope 123. Par for the course is 72, course record stands at 63.

68

Bing Maloney Golf Course

6801 Freeport Blvd.
Sacramento, CA 95822

(916) 428-9401

18 Hole Course

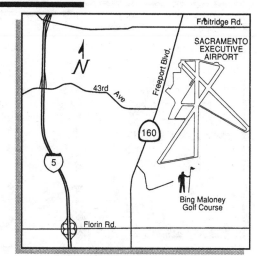

Green Fees:

	Weekdays	Weekends
9 Holes:	$7.00	$8.00
18 Holes:	$11.50	$14.00
Twilight Rate:	$7.00	$8.00
Senior Discount: $8.00		

Outfitting:

Golf Cars - 9 Holes: $8.00   Golf Cars - 18 Holes: $16.00
Pull Carts: $2.00   Clubs: $10.00

Lessons & More:

Club Pro: Tom E. Doris   Lessons: $25 / Lesson
This course offers a Practice Putting Green and a Driving Range.
Bucket prices: $2.00 - $3.50. They provide a full restaurant that
is open from dawn to dusk and a Pro Shop with an extensive
inventory of golf equipment. Reservations can be made one
week in advance. Their busiest day of the week is Saturday,
least busy day is Tuesday.

Facts & Figures:

There are over 100,000 rounds of golf played each year on this
busy 18 hole golf course which opened in 1952. The course
measures 6281 yards from the Championship Tees, rated 69.7
with a par of 72. From the Ladies' Tees it is 5972 yards long,
rated 72.6, slope 119 and par is 73. The course is flat so your lies
will be good provided you stay within the narrow fairways. The
small greens insist upon accurate approach shots. Water can only
slow you down on one hole.

Sacramento County

Campus Commons Golf Course

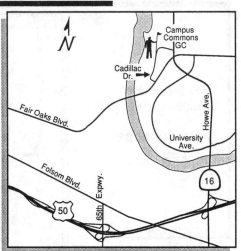

2 Cadillac Drive
Sacramento, CA 95825

(916) 922-5861

9 Hole Course

Green Fees:

	Weekdays	Weekends
9 Holes:	$6.50	$7.50
18 Holes:	$10.50	$11.50

Twilight Rate: n.a.
Senior Discount: n.a.

Outfitting:

Golf Cars- 9 Holes: $8.00		Golf Cars - 18 Holes:
Pull Carts: $1.50		Clubs: $5.00

Lessons & More:

Club Pro: Mike Fanccolli   Lessons: $25 / 30 Minutes
There is a only a Practice Putting Green here at Campus Commons Golf Course. Their new facilities includes a Clubhouse, Snack Bar and Pro Shop. Reservations can be made one week in advance. Their busiest day of the week is Sunday.

Facts & Figures:

Campus Commons Golf Course opened 20 years ago. It is a 9 hole, par 3 course that runs along the bank of the American River. The hilly, treed landscape provides a course that is easy to walk and play. The Men's rating is 54, the Ladies' is 56. Total yardage from the Men's Tees is 1673, from the Ladies' it is 1508. Par for the course is 29.

Cherry Island Golf Course

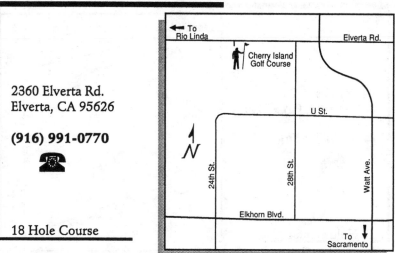

2360 Elverta Rd.
Elverta, CA 95626

(916) 991-0770

18 Hole Course

Green Fees:

	Weekdays	Weekends
9 Holes:	$9.50	n.a.
18 Holes:	$15.50	$18.00
Twilight Rate:	$9.50	$10.75

Senior Discount: With senior resident card

Outfitting:

Golf Cars - 9 Holes: $12.00   Golf Cars - 18 Holes: $18.00
Pull Carts: $2.00   Clubs: $10.00

Lessons & More:

Club Pro: Blair Kline   Lessons: $25 / 30 Minutes*
Cherry Island offers a Practice Putting Green, a Chipping Green and a Driving Range. Bucket prices: $2.00 - $4.00. They provide a full restaurant and lounge and a Pro Shop which carries an extensive inventory of golf equipment. Reservations for the weekend can be made on the Monday prior. *Rick Graham is the teaching professional. Residents of Sacramento county receive a discount on Green Fees.

Facts & Figures:

This new, 18 hole, championship course opened in June of 1990 and is a lovely addition to the area. Designed by Robert Muir Graves, it features water hazards, mature oak trees, rolling bentgrass greens and bluegrass fairways. Be prepared to use all the clubs in your bag, this is a real strategy course. There are four sets of tees, Blue, White, Gold and Red. The yardages are 6562, 6201, 5556 and 5163, respectively. Overall par is 72.

71

Cordova Golf Course

9425 Jackson Rd.
Sacramento, CA 95826

(916) 362-1196

☎

18 Hole Course

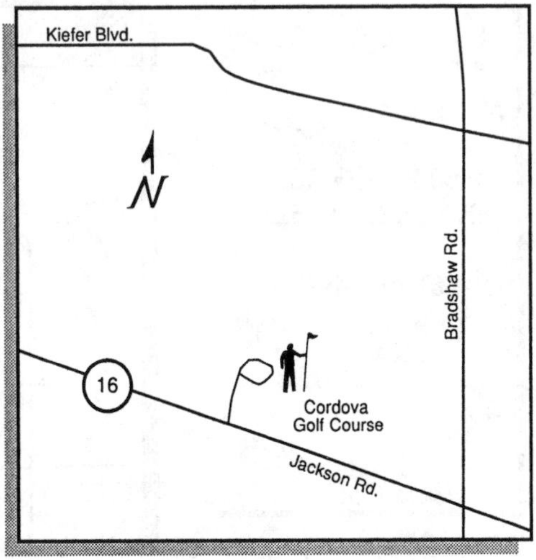

Green Fees:

	Weekdays	Weekends
9 Holes:	$3.00	$3.50
18 Holes:	$5.00	$6.00

Twilight Rate: n.a.
Senior Discount: Less 20%

Outfitting:

Golf Cars- 9 Holes: $6.00   Golf Cars - 18 Holes: $12.00
Pull Carts: $2.00   Clubs: $6.00

Lessons & More:

Club Pro: Jim Marta   Lessons: $25.00
There is a Practice Putting Green and Driving Range available at
Cordova Golf Course. Bucket prices: $2.00 - $3.00. There is a
Snack Bar open from 7 a.m. until 8 p.m. for your convenience. A
complete Pro Shop is also available. Reservations can be made
one week in advance. Their least busy day is Monday. The
Driving Range is open till 10:00 p.m. March thru November.

Facts & Figures:

Cordova Golf Course is a short 18 hole course that measures
4755 yards from the Men's Tees and 4728 from the Ladies'. Par
for the Men is 63, it is rated 61, slope is 90. Ladies' Par is 66,
rated 64.9, slope is 96. The course is flat making it easy to walk.
The greens are small and the fairways, lined with plenty of trees,
are narrow. You will encounter water on three of the holes. The
course is not difficult. There is only 1 par 5 hole, 7 par 4 holes
and 10 par 3's. Good beginners course.

Davis Municipal Golf Course

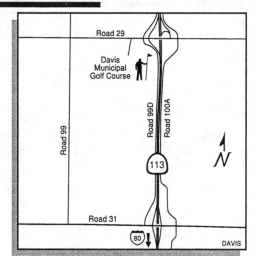

Rd. 29, Hwy. 113
Davis, CA 95617

(916) 756-4010

18 Hole Course

Green Fees:

	Weekdays	Weekends
9 Holes:	n.a.	n.a.
18 Holes:	$10.00	$11.00

Twilight Rate: $6.00
Senior Discount: $7.00 weekdays only

Outfitting:

Golf Cars - 9 Holes: n.a.	Golf Cars - 18 Holes: $15.00
Pull Carts: $1.50	Clubs: $4.00 / $7.00

Lessons & More:

Club Pro: Jerry Lilliedoll   **Lessons:** $20 / 30 Minutes
Davis Golf Course provides two Practice Putting Greens and a Driving Range. Bucket prices: $1.50 - $3.00. They have a Snack Bar open from dawn until dusk. The Pro Shop will be able to help fill most of your golfing needs. Reservations can be made one week in advance.

Facts & Figures:

Davis Golf Course is known to be easy to walk as well as easy to play. It is located in open country, surrounded by farm land. As you might guess, it is pretty flat, but the tree lined fairways and 2 water hazards turn it into a pleasant 18 hole course. It is 4998 yards long from the Men's Tees and rated 63.4. From the Ladies' Tees it is 4445 yards long and rated 60.9. There are no par 5 holes and 6 of the holes are par 3's. Par for the course is 66/67. Course record stands at 56.

Diamond Oaks Municipal Golf Course

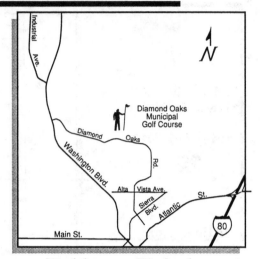

349 Diamond Oaks Rd.
Roseville, CA 95678

(916) 783-4947

18 Hole Course

Green Fees:

	Weekdays	Weekends
9 Holes:	$7.50	$8.00
18 Holes:	$13.00	$14.00

Twilight Rate: $6.50
Senior Discount: Residents of Roseville only

Outfitting:

Golf Cars- 9 Holes: $8.00	Golf Cars - 18 Holes:$16.00
Pull Carts: $1.00 / 9 Holes	Clubs: $5.00 / $10.00

Lessons & More:

Club Pro: Ed Vasconcellos   Lessons: $25 / 30 Minutes
There are two Practice Putting Greens and a Driving Range
available. Bucket prices: $2.00 - $3.50. They provide a full
restaurant and a Snack Bar, open from dawn to dusk. Their new
Pro Shop carries an extensive inventory of golf equipment.
Reservations can be made one week in advance for weekdays,
and on Monday prior, beginning at 7 a.m. by phone, or 6:45 a.m.
in person, for weekends.

Facts & Figures:

This municipal, 18 hole, golf course opened in 1963. It is a lovely
rolling course with plenty of oak trees lining the wide, forgiving
fairways. It presents a challenge to every experienced level of
golfers. The course measures 6283 yards from the Championship
Tees, 6065 from the Men's Tees and 5608 from the Ladies'.
Men's Par is 72, slope 110, Ladies' Par is 73, slope 112.

Dry Creek Ranch Golf Course

809 Crystal Way
Galt, CA 95632

(209) 745-2330

18 Hole Course

Green Fees:

	Weekdays	Weekends
9 Holes:	$7.00	$12.00
18 Holes:	$14.00	$24.00

Twilight Rate: n.a.
Senior Discount: n.a.

Outfitting:

Golf Cars - 9 Holes: $9.00   Golf Cars - 18 Holes: $18.00
Pull Carts: $2.00   Clubs: $10.00

Lessons & More:

Club Pro: Rod Sims   Lessons: $20 / Lesson
A Practice Putting Green and a Driving Range are available.
Bucket prices: $1.25 - $2.00. Their Snack Bar is open from 9 a.m.
until 9 p.m. Their "Golden Acorn" restaurant is also available.
The Pro Shop carries an extensive inventory of golf equipment to
help fill your golfing needs. You can reserve Tee Times two
weeks in advance.

Facts & Figures:

Jack Fleming designed Dry Creek Ranch which opened in 1962.
The name of the course is deceiving, bringing your ball retriever
is recommended. If the water doesn't cause problems then the
towering oak trees might. The slope ratings are: Blue 129, White
126 and Red 128. It is in excellent condition.

Sacramento County

75

El Dorado Hills Golf Course

3775 El Dorado Hills Blvd.
El Dorado Hills, CA 95630

(916) 933-6552

18 Hole Course

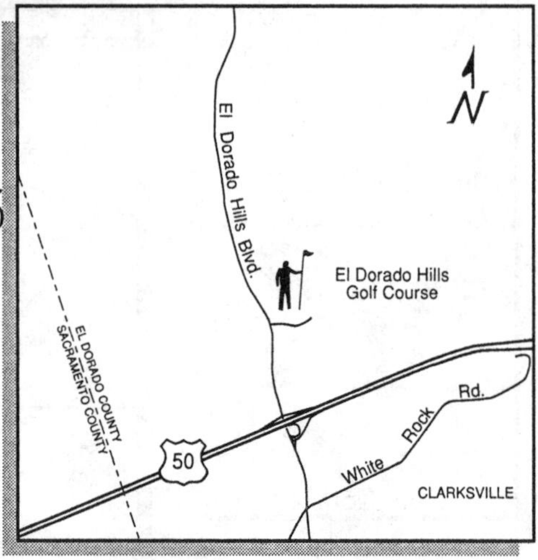

Green Fees:

	Weekdays	Weekends
9 Holes:	$9.00	$12.00
18 Holes:	$16.00	$20.00

Twilight Rate: $4.00
Senior Discount: With monthly passes

Outfitting:

Golf Cars- 9 Holes: *$10/$12   Golf Cars - 18 Holes: *$16/$18
Pull Carts: $3 / 9 Holes   Clubs: $5.00

Lessons & More:

Club Pro: Ted Fitzpatrick   **Lessons:** $20 / 30 Minutes
El Dorado Hills provides a Practice Putting Green, Chipping
Green and a Driving Range. Bucket prices: $1.50 - $3.00. Their
Snack Bar, which features a great breakfast, is open from 5 a.m.
until 10 p.m. The Pro Shop can fill your immediate golfing
needs. Weekend reservations can be made seven days in advance, weekday reservations can be made two weeks ahead. The
fees following Golf Cars designate weekday and weekend rates.

Facts & Figures:

This eighteen hole course, designed by Robert Trent, Sr., has
been in operation since 1962. This is a short 18 hole course.
From the White Tees it plays for a total of 4233 yards and is rated
58.3, slope is 93. Par for the course is 61, course record stands at
54. The course is rolling and wooded. There are water hazards
on 11 of the holes, so bring along a few extra balls. This is a
difficult course, a test of your golfing abilities.

Foothill Golf Center

7000 Verner Ave.
Sacramento, CA 95841

(916) 725-3355

9 Hole Course

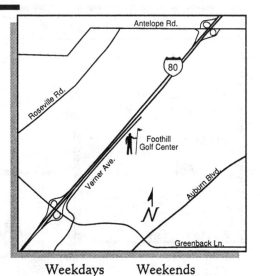

Green Fees:

	Weekdays	Weekends
9 Holes:	$4.25	$4.75
18 Holes:	$7.75	$8.50

Twilight Rate: n.a.
Senior Discount: n.a.

Outfitting:

Golf Cars - 9 Holes: n.a.	Golf Cars - 18 Holes: n.a.
Pull Carts: $1.25	Clubs: $2.50

Lessons & More:

Club Pro: Paul Ottaviano   Lessons: $20 / 45 Minutes
Foothill Golf Center provides a Practice Putting Green and a
Chipping Green. Their restaurant is open daily from dawn to
dusk. Their Pro Shop carries a limited amount of golf merchandise. They do not take reservations.

Facts & Figures:

Foothill Golf Center was designed with the beginner golfer in
mind. It is the shortest course in Sacramento and free of any
hazards. The longest hole is only 148 yards long and the average
hole length is 120 yards.

Sacramento County

77

Haggin Oaks Municipal Golf Course

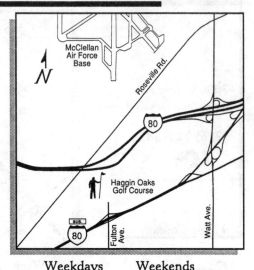

3645 Fulton Ave.
Sacramento, CA 95821

(916) 481-4507

36 Hole Course

Green Fees:

	Weekdays	Weekends
9 Holes:	$5.75	$7.00
18 Holes:	$11.50	$14.00

Twilight Rate: $7.00
Senior Discount: $9.25 for residents of Sacramento

Outfitting:

Golf Cars- 9 Holes: $8.00	Golf Cars - 18 Holes: $16.00
Pull Carts: $2.00	Clubs: $7.50

Lessons & More:

Club Pro: Ken Morton   Lessons: $30 / 30 Minutes
Haggin Oaks offers a Practice Putting Green, a Chipping Green and a Driving Range. Bucket prices: $2.00 - $3.50. They have a Snack Bar that is open from dawn to dusk and a large Pro Shop for your convenience. Reservations can be made for the weekends by calling on the Tuesday morning prior and weekday reservations can be made one week in advance.

Facts & Figures:

Haggin Oaks Golf Course consists of two 18 hole courses. The North Course was designed by Alister Mckenzie between 1957-1959, and the South Course designed by Mike McDonough in 1932. The courses are fairly flat with tree lined fairways and average size greens. Arcade Creek winds its way throughout the course. The South Course measures 6287 yards long and is rated 69.1. The Championship North Course measures 6860 yards and is rated 71.4. Par for both courses is 72. The record low score for the South Course is 63 and for the North Course it is 64. This is a great value facility.

78

Lighthouse Golf & Country Club

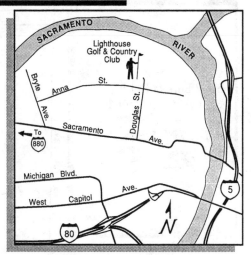

500 Douglas Street
West Sacramento, CA
95605

(916) 372-4949

18 Hole Course

Green Fees:

	Weekdays	Weekends
9 Holes:	$10.00	n.a.
18 Holes:	$15.00	$20.00
Twilight Rate:	$10.00	$12.00
Senior Discount:	$12.00 Weekdays only	

Outfitting:

Golf Cars - 9 Holes: $8.00	Golf Cars - 18 Holes: $16.00
Pull Carts: $2.00	Clubs: $10.00

Lessons & More:

Club Pro: Robert Halpenny   Lessons: $25 / Lesson
A Practice Putting Green, Chipping Green and a Driving Range
are available. Bucket price: $2.00. They have a Snack Bar
available. The Pro Shop carries an extensive golf inventory.
Reservations can be made seven days in advance. Their busiest
day of the week is Saturday, least busy on Monday.

Facts & Figures:

This new 18 hole public course, designed by Bert Stamps, opened
in May of 1990. It is the centerpiece of the Lighthouse Marina
Development located across the river from downtown Sacramento. The course measures just slightly over 4700 yards from
the Blue Tees, is rated 64.0, Men's Par is 65. From the White
Tees it is rated 62.8 and from the Red is rated 62.5. The fairly flat
fairways wind their way through a variety of trees and several
lakes. There is enough of a challenge here to satisfy most golfers.

Roseville Rolling Greens Golf Course

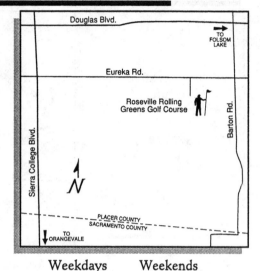

5572 Eureka Road
Roseville, CA 95661

(916) 797-9986

9 Hole Course

Green Fees:

	Weekdays	Weekends
9 Holes:	$7.00	$8.00
18 Holes:	$11.00	$13.00

Twilight Rate: n.a.
Senior Discount: n.a.

Outfitting:

Golf Cars- 9 Holes: n.a.   Golf Cars - 18 Holes: n.a.
Pull Carts: $2.00   Clubs: n.a.

Lessons & More:

Club Pro: Lessons: Available

Roseville Rolling Greens offers a Practice Putting Green as their warm-up facility. They have a Snack Bar open from dawn to dusk and a small Pro Shop. The course does not take reservations, first come, first served. If you are interested in golf lessons, please contact the Pro Shop.

Facts & Figures:

This often played, executive 9 hole course has been open for the past 40 years. The many sand traps and water hazards add to the difficulty of this pleasant to play course. The name "Rolling Greens" best describes the terrain. Total yardage is 1500, par is 27. Course records are 24 for 9 holes and 50 for 18 holes.

William Land Park Golf Course

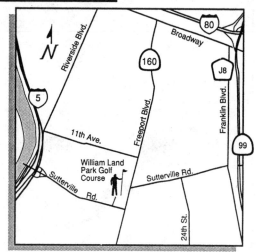

1701 Sutterville Rd.
Sacramento, CA 95831

(916) 455-5014

9 Hole Course

Green Fees:

	Weekdays	Weekends
9 Holes:	$5.75	$7.00
18 Holes:		

Twilight Rate: n.a.
Senior Discount: $4.50

Outfitting:

Golf Cars - 9 Holes: n.a.   Golf Cars - 18 Holes: n.a.
Pull Carts: $1.00   Clubs: $5.00

Lessons & More:

Club Pro: Steve Feliciano   Lessons: $25 / Lesson
William Land Park Golf Course offers a Practice Putting Green and a Chipping Green as warm-up facilities. Their Snack Bar is open from dawn to dusk. The Pro Shop can help fill most of your golfing needs. Reservations can be made one week in advance. Their busiest day of the week is Saturday, least busy day is Tuesday.

Facts & Figures:

This nine hole course has been in operation since 1929. It plays for 2600 yards and has a par of 34. There is one par 5 hole, three par 3 holes and the rest are par 4's. It is rated 63 if played twice and the Women's slope is 100. Course record for 18 holes is 59. Their big greens give an advantage to the golfers who are still working on their approach shots.

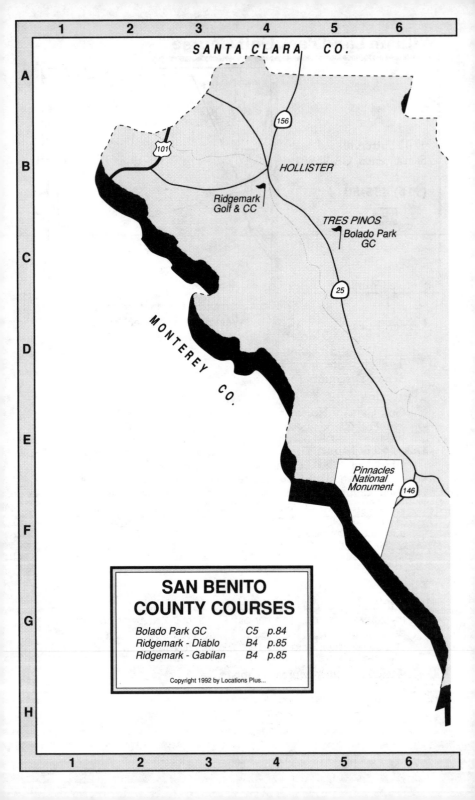

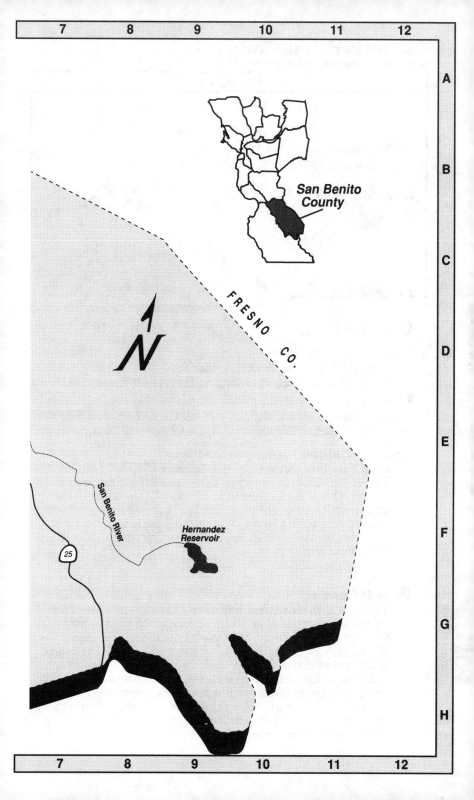

Bolado Park Golf Course

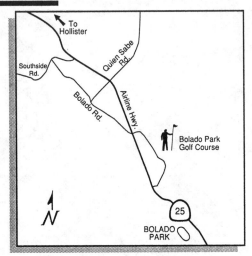

7777 Airline Highway
Tres Pinos, CA 95075

(408) 628-9995

9 Hole Course

Green Fees:

	Weekdays	Weekends
9 Holes:	*$10.00	*$15.00
18 Holes:		
Twilight Rate: After 3 p.m.	$8.00	$12.00

Senior Discount: $8.00 - Monday, Thursday & Friday

Outfitting:

Golf Cars - 9 Holes: $10.00	Golf Cars - 18 Holes: $20.00
Pull Carts: $2.00	Clubs: $2.00

Lessons & More:

Club Pro: Bob Trevino   **Lessons:** $20 / 30 Minutes* *
Bolado Park Golf Course offers a Practice Putting Green and a
Driving Range. Bucket prices: $1.50 - $2.50. The Snack Bar is
open from 7 a.m. until 7 p.m. The Pro Shop will help you fill
most of your golfing needs. The teaching pro is Lary Philbrick.
They do not take reservations, first come, first served. ***Green
Fees allow all day play.**

Facts & Figures:

This well maintained, nine hole course has a separate set of tees
for playing a second nine. Total yardage for 18 holes is 5986
from the Men's Tees and 5636 yards from the Ladies' Tees.
Course ratings are 67.5 and 71.5, respectively. Par for the course
is 70. It is a full nine holes with all the features you would expect
to find on a regulation 18 hole course. The fairways are lined by
many large trees making it difficult to cross over to another hole.
It is a lovely course nestled up against the foothills. They regularly host the Hooper Tournament in June and the Trevino
Tournament in September.

Ridgemark Golf & Country Club

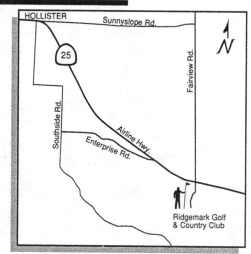

3800 Airline Highway
Hollister, CA 95023

(408) 637-1010

36 Hole Course

Green Fees:

	Weekdays	Weekends
9 Holes:	$20.00	$28.00
18 Holes:	$12.00	$15.00

Twilight Rates: n.a.
Senior Discount:

Outfitting:

Golf Cars - 9 Holes:	Golf Cars - 18 Holes: $20.00
Pull Carts: $2.00	Clubs: $20.00

Lessons & More:

Club Pro: Kathy Wake   Lessons: $25 / 30 Minutes
Ridgemark Golf & Country Club offers Practice Putting Green, a
Chipping Green and a Driving Range. Bucket prices: $2.00 -
$4.00. They have 2 outside Snack Bars, an in-door grill plus a full
restaurant and lounge. The Pro Shop is complete. All reservations
can be made seven days in advance beginning at 6:30 a.m. This
is a semi-private facility, public access to each course alternates
daily.

Facts & Figures:

The Diablo and the Gabilan are the two 18 hole courses here at
Ridgemark. The Diablo Course is 6603 yards from the Men's
Blue Tees, is rated 71.9, slope 123. It runs along the foothills and
the golfer is challenged by tight fairways and strategic pin
placement. The Gabilan is the longer course measuring 6671
yards from the Men's Blue Tees and is rated 72.0, slope 124. This
course is nearly surrounded by neighboring homes, each hole
offers striking views of the Gabilan Mountain range.

San Benito County

85

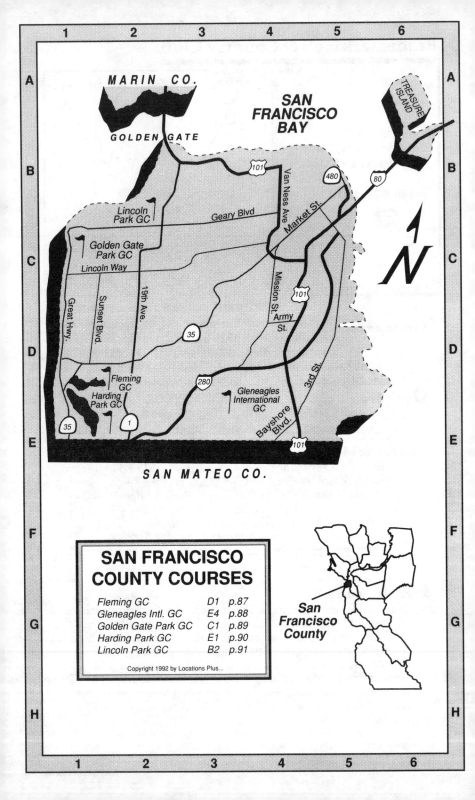

SAN FRANCISCO
BAY

MARIN CO.

GOLDEN GATE

TREASURE ISLAND

Lincoln Park GC

Geary Blvd

Van Ness Ave

Market St.

Golden Gate Park GC

Lincoln Way

Great Hwy.

Sunset Blvd.

19th Ave.

Mission St.

Army St.

101

3rd St.

Fleming GC

Harding Park GC

Gleneagles International GC

Bayshore Blvd.

SAN MATEO CO.

SAN FRANCISCO COUNTY COURSES

Fleming GC	*D1*	*p.87*
Gleneagles Intl. GC	*E4*	*p.88*
Golden Gate Park GC	*C1*	*p.89*
Harding Park GC	*E1*	*p.90*
Lincoln Park GC	*B2*	*p.91*

Copyright 1992 by Locations Plus...

San Francisco County

Fleming Golf Course

Harding Road at
   Skyline Blvd.
San Francisco, CA 94132

(415) 661-1865

9 Hole Course

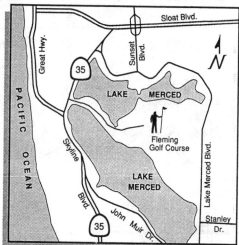

Green Fees:

	Weekdays	Weekends
9 Holes:	$9.00	$10.00
18 Holes:	$18.00	$20.00
Twilight Rate:	$8.00	$10.00

Senior Discount: Restricted to San Francisco residents

Outfitting:

Golf Car - 9 Holes: $10.00   Golf Car - 18 Holes: $18.00
      Pull Carts: $3.00   Clubs: $10.00

Lessons & More:

Club Pro: David Mutton   **Lessons:** $30 / 30 Minutes
Fleming Golf Course offers a Practice Putting Green and a Driving
Range. Bucket prices: $3 to $5. Their restaurant, "Benny's", is
open from 7 a.m. till dark, a lounge is also available. The Golf
Shop is complete. They do not accept reservations, first come,
first served.

Facts & Figures:

This executive 9 hole course was designed by Jack Fleming nearly
60 years ago. Every hole on this slightly rolling course is surrounded by lovely old pine trees. There are 2316 yards of play to
the course, par is 32. The holes consist of one par 5 hole at 460
yards, three par 4 holes and the par 3 holes range from 150 to 220
yards long. The course is rated 31.3. Most golfers will be
pleased with the wide variety offered by this nine hole course.
Fleming Golf Course is part of the Harding Park Complex which
consists of 27 holes.

San Francisco County

Gleneagles International Golf Course

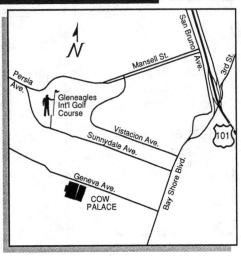

2100 Sunnydale Avenue
San Francisco, CA 94134

(415) 587-2425

9 Hole Course

Green Fees:

	Weekdays	Weekends
9 Holes:	$9.00	n.a.
18 Holes:	$15.00	$20.00

Twilight Rate: n.a.
Senior Discount: n.a.

Outfitting:

Golf Car - 9 Holes: $10.00	Golf Car - 18 Holes: $20.00
Pull Carts: n.a.	Clubs: n.a.

Lessons & More:

Club Pro: Mick Soli   **Lessons:** n.a.

There is a Practice Putting Green, but no Chipping Green or Driving Range available at Gleneagles. Their restaurant, "Old Peculiar's Public House", is open from dawn to dusk. A cocktail lounge is also available. Reservations are only taken for weekends and holidays on the Monday prior, beginning at 7:00 a.m. Metal spike shoes are required on the course.

Fact & Figures:

The course originally opened in 1962. It was rebuilt in 1980 and since then it has been rated one of the toughest 9 hole courses in California. It has a separate set of tees for playing a second nine holes. In 1985 The National Golf Foundation found this course to be among one of the 3 best 9 hole courses in the United States. The course was designed by Jack Fleming who also designed the Cypress Point Golf Course. Total yardage is 3293, course par is 36. There are 2 par 5's, 2 par 3's and the rest are par 4's. Course rating is 71.1 and slope is 129.

Golden Gate Park Golf Course

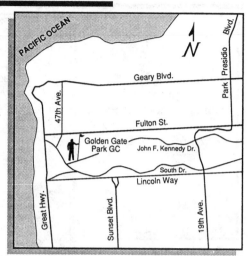

47th Avenue
and Fulton Street
San Francisco, CA 94121

(415) 751-8987

9 Hole Course

Green Fees:

	Weekdays	Weekends
9 Holes:	$6.00	$9.00
18 Holes:	$12.00	$18.00

Twilight Rate: n.a.
Senior Discount: Residents of San Francisco only

Outfitting:

Golf Car - 9 Holes:	Golf Car - 18 Holes: $8.00
Pull Carts: $3.50	Clubs: $6.

Lessons & More:

Club Pro: Jim Ross   Lessons: Available
There is a Practice Putting Green available at Golden Gate Park
Golf Course, but no Chipping Green or Driving Range. Thiggy's
Restaurant is open daily from 6 a.m. until sunset, beer and wine
are also available. The Pro Shop will help in filling your immediate golfing needs. They do not take reservations, first come, first
served.

Facts & Figures:

The beautiful Golden Gate Park is the setting for this 9 hole, par 3
golf course. It plays for only 1357 yards, the longest hole
measuring 193 yards and the shortest 113. This conveniently
located course allows for a good iron workout. The beginning
golfer will enjoy the relaxed atmosphere the Golden Gate Park
Golf Course offers.

Harding Park Golf Course

Harding Road at
   Skyline Blvd.
San Francisco, CA 94132

(415) 664-4690
☎

18 Hole Course

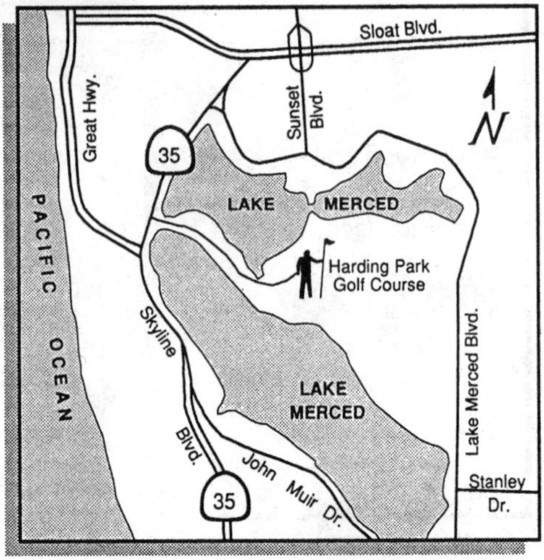

Green Fees:

	Weekdays	Weekends
9 Holes:	*$8.00	*$11.00
18 Holes:	$15.00	$20.00
Twilight Rate:	$8.00	$10.00

Senior Discount: San Francisco residents only

Outfitting:

Golf Car - 9 Holes: $10.00   Golf Car - 18 Holes: $18.00
Pull Carts: $3.00   Clubs: $10.00

Lessons & More:

Club Pro: David Mutton   **Lessons:** $30 / 30 Minutes
Harding Park Golf Course offers a Practice Putting Green and a
Driving Range. Bucket prices: $3 - $5. Their restaurant and
lounge "Benny's" is open from 7 a.m. till dark. The Golf Shop is
complete. Weekday reservations can be made one week in
advance. Weekend reservations can be made by SF City residents, Tues. for Sat. and Wed. for Sun. at 6:00 a.m. ***9 Hole
rates apply before 8:00 a.m. only.**

Fact & Figures:

The course has been in operation since 1925. In 1963-1968 the
course played host to the Lucky Open on the PGA Tour and in
1981 the Eureka Senior Tour Event. This beautiful course,
located in San Francisco, has its boundaries set by a lake on 6 of
its holes. This course is long, 6586 yards from the Men's Tees,
Par 72, and 6187 yards from the Women's Tees, Par 73. Fleming
Golf Course, a nine hole par 32 executive course, is part of this
golf complex.

Lincoln Park Golf Course

34th Ave. and Clement St.
San Francisco, CA 94121

(415) 221-9911

18 Hole Course

Green Fees:

	Weekdays	Weekends
9 Holes:	n.a.	n.a.
18 Holes:	$15.00	$19.00
Twilight Rate:	$8.00	$10.00
Senior Discount:	San Francisco residents only	

Outfitting:

Golf Car - 9 Holes:	$10.00	Golf Car - 18 Holes:	$18.00
Pull Carts:	$3.00	Clubs:	$10.00

Lessons & More:

Club Pro: John Constantine   **Lessons:** $25 / 30 Minutes
Lincoln Park Golf Course offers a Practice Putting Green, but no Chipping Green or Driving Range. Thiggy's Restaurant is open from 6:30 a.m. till 12:00. A cocktail lounge is also available. Weekend reservations can be made three days in advance, and one day in advance for weekdays.

Facts & Figures:

Lincoln Park Golf Course originally opened with just 6 holes, in 1916 it was expanded to include 18 holes. This golf course is uniquely set around the Legion of Honor Art Museum, overlooking the Pacific Ocean. From this vantage point, you will be able to enjoy many splendid views of San Francisco while playing this lovely course. Be sure to bring along a light jacket or windbreaker to ward off any chilling winds swirling up from the Gate. The Men's course rating is 65.3, the Women's is 68.2. Total yardage from the Men's Tees is 5149, Par 68. Total yardage from the Women's Tees is 4984, Par 70.

San Francisco County

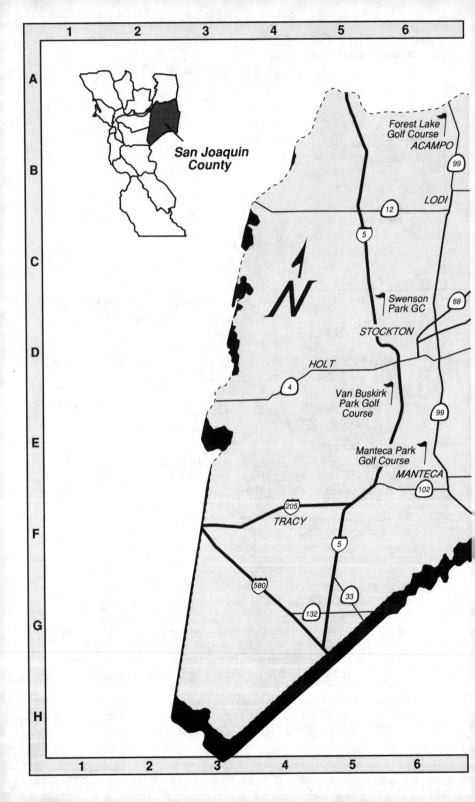

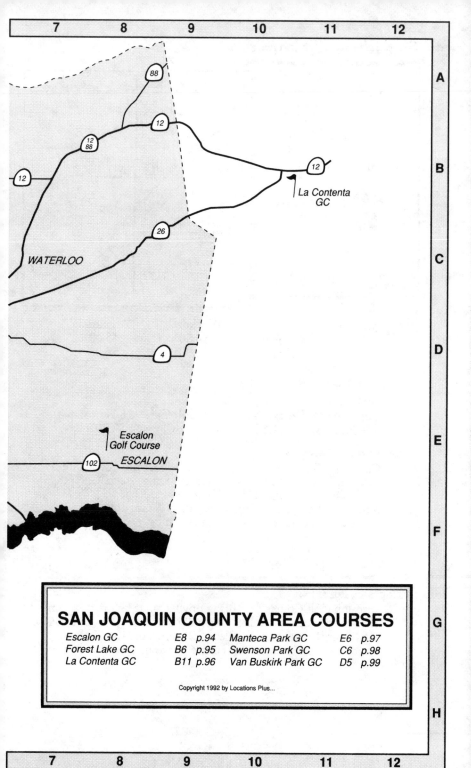

SAN JOAQUIN COUNTY AREA COURSES

Escalon Golf Course

17051 S. Escalon-Bellota
                    Road
Escalon, CA 95320

(209) 838-1277

☎

9 Hole Course

Green Fees:

	Weekdays	Weekends
9 Holes:	$4.50	$5.00
18 Holes:	$8.00	$9.00

Twilight Rate: n.a.
Senior Discount: n.a.

Outfitting:

Golf Cars - 9 Holes: n.a.	Golf Cars - 18 Holes: n.a.
Pull Carts: $1.50	Clubs: $2.00

Lessons & More:

Club Pro: Tony Hall   Lessons: $25 / 60 Minutes
Escalon Golf Course offers a Practice Putting Green, Chipping
Green and a Driving Range. Bucket prices: $2.50 - $1.25. They
provide a Snack Bar which is open from 7 a.m. until dark, 7 days
a week. Reservations for Tee Times can be made at any time.

Facts & Figures:

Escalon Golf Course was first a driving range before it became
this short, but enjoyable 9 hole golf course. It plays for a total of
1520 yards. The longest hole is 250 yards, the shortest is 70
yards. It is an intermediate course not to be taken too lightly.

Forest Lake Golf Course

2450 Woodson Rd.
Acampo, CA 95220

(209) 369-5451

18 Hole Course

(Map showing Forest Lake Golf Course location with Liberty Rd., Route 99, N. Cherokee Rd., Lower Sacramento Rd., Collier Rd., Calimyrna Rd., Woodson Rd., and Jahant Rd.)

Green Fees:

	Weekdays	Weekends
9 Holes:	$5.00	$7.00
18 Holes:	$7.00	$9.00

Twilight Rate: n.a.
Senior Discount: n.a.

Outfitting:

Golf Cars - 9 Holes: $7.00	Golf Cars - 18 Holes: $12.00
Pull Carts: $1.25	Clubs: $2.00

Lessons & More:

Club Pro: David Ring   **Lessons:** $20 / 45 Minutes
Forest Lake Golf Course provides a Practice Putting Green, Chipping Green, Sand Trap and a Driving Range. Bucket price: $1.00. Their Snack Bar and Pro Shop are open from dawn to dusk, daily. Reservations can be made one week in advance. Their least busy day of the week is Tuesday.

Fact & Figures:

This is a lovely, well established, executive 18 hole course which has been in operation for the past 35 years. They have recently included additional holes that will vary the 18 holes in play. The course now measures 5000 yards, and par for the course is 66. The many mature trees lining the fairways can become formidable obstacles if straight hitting is not yet a developed skill.

La Contenta Golf Club

1653 Highway 26
Valley Springs, CA 95252

(209) 772-1081

18 Hole Course

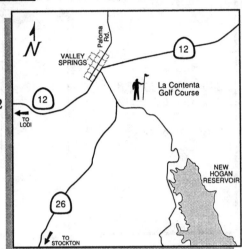

Green Fees:

	Weekdays	Weekends
9 Holes:	n.a.	n.a.
18 Holes:	$16.00	$26.00
Twilight Rate:	$9.00	$13.00
Senior Discount:	$11.00 Monday - Thursday	

Outfitting:

Golf Cars - 9 Holes: n.a.   Golf Cars - 18 Holes: $18.00
Pull Carts: $2.00   Clubs: $10.00

Lessons & More:

Club Pro: Glen Reynolds   Lessons: Yes
La Contenta Golf Club offers a Practice Putting Green, Chipping
Green and a netted hitting area. Their newly expanded facility
consists of a Clubhouse, restaurant and a Pro Shop that will meet
the needs of the golfers. Reservations can be made two weeks in
advance.

Facts & Figures:

This is a 18 hole, semi-private, course that provides a challenging
game of golf, as well as an enjoyable outing. The course measures 6500 yards and has a par of 72. It is a tight, rolling course
bordered by homes on some of the holes, and sprinkled with
streams and lakes on others. Their hole #13, which is a par 3, 175
yards is most memorable. The hole is quite scenic and often
featured in Northern California golf articles. The course is in the
best shape ever.

Manteca Park Golf Course

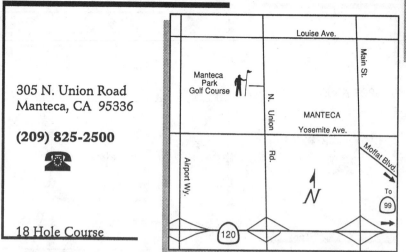

305 N. Union Road
Manteca, CA 95336

(209) 825-2500

18 Hole Course

Green Fees:

	Weekdays	Weekends
9 Holes:	$7.00	$8.00
18 Holes:	$10.75	$14.25

Twilight Rate: $7.00
Senior Discount: $3.00 after 11:00 p.m. on Tuesdays only.

Outfitting:

Golf Cars - 9 Holes: $10.00   Golf Cars - 18 Holes: $18.00
    Pull Carts: $2.00   Clubs: $8.00

Lessons & More:

Club Pro: Alan Thomas   Lessons: $25.00
There is a Practice Putting Green and a Driving Range available.
Bucket prices: $2.50 - $4.00. Their new Clubhouse is open from
7 a.m. until 7 p.m. for you convenience. The Pro Shop's inventory is extensive. Reservations can be made 7 days in advance for weekdays and on the Monday prior for the weekends. This 18 hole course is busiest on Saturdays.

Fact & Figures:

Manteca Park Golf Course opened in 1966 with 9 holes and in 1978 added an additional 9. The fairways are narrow, the rough is thick and there are lateral water hazards on seven of the holes. Yardages range from 6447 from the Championship Tees, 6281 from the Regular Tees and 5739 from the Ladies' Tees. The course is rated 70.2, 69.2 and 72.1, respectively. Par is 72.

Swenson Park Golf Course

6803 Alexandria Pl.
Stockton, CA 95207

(209) 477-0774

27 Hole Course

(Map showing Mosher Slough, Thornton Rd, Hammer Ln., Pershing Ave., Fivemile Slough, Alexandria Pl., Swenson Park Golf Course, Benjamin Holt Dr., Highway 5)

Green Fees:

	Weekdays	Weekends
9 Holes:	$6.00	$6.50
18 Holes:	$9.00	$10.00

Twilight Rate: $1.00 off
Senior Discount: $4.50 after 11:00 - with monthly card

Outfitting:

Golf Cars - 9 Holes: $10.00   Golf Cars - 18 Holes: $18.00
    Pull Carts: $1.50   Clubs: $7.00

Lessons & More:

Club Pro: Ernie George   Lessons: $25 / 45 Minutes
There is a Practice Putting Green, Chipping Green and a Driving
Range at Swenson Park. Bucket Prices: $1.50 - $3.00. Their
Snack Bar is open from 6 a.m. until 6 p.m. daily. Their Pro Shop
is complete. Weekend reservations can be made early on the
Monday prior, for weekdays 7 days in advance. They are busiest
on the weekends, least busy on Mondays and Tuesdays.

Facts & Figures:

Swenson Park has been in operation since 1950. They have an
executive 9 hole, par 3 course that plays for 1380 yards in
addition to a regulation 18 hole. There are plenty of trees on the
course and you will find a lot of elevated greens. The 18 hole
course is rated 69.1, slope is 110. Total yards from the Men's
Tees is 6407, par is 72. From the Women's Tees it is 6266 and
par is 74.

Van Buskirk Park Golf Course

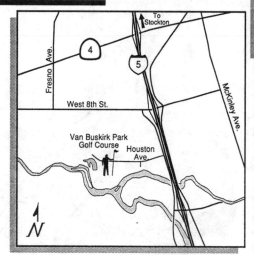

1740 Houston Ave.
Stockton, CA 95206

(209) 464-5629

18 Hole Course

Green Fees:

	Weekdays	Weekends
9 Holes:	n.a.	n.a.
18 Holes:	$9.00	$10.00

Twilight Rate: $7.50
Senior Discount: $6.50 after 11:00 p.m.

Outfitting:

Golf Cars - 9 Holes: $10.00	Golf Cars - 18 Holes: $18.00
Pull Carts: $2.00	Clubs: $3.00

Lessons & More:

Club Pro: Jose Santiago   Lessons: $20 / 30 Minutes
There is a new Practice Putting Green and a Driving Range
available at Van Buskirk Golf Course. A bucket of balls is $2.00.
Their Snack Bar is open from 6 a.m. until 6 p.m. There is also a
Pro Shop to help fill your immediate golfing needs. Golf reserva-
tions can be made one week in advance for weekdays and on the
Monday prior for the weekend.

Fact & Figures:

This 18 hole course is owned by the City of Stockton Depart-
ment of Parks & Recreation. It runs along the San Joaquin River
which adds to the pleasantness of the course. It plays fairly long
with 6572 yards from the Men's Tees and 6200 from the Ladies'.
It is rated 69.3, par 72 for the Men and 73.5, par 74, slope 114 for
the Ladies.

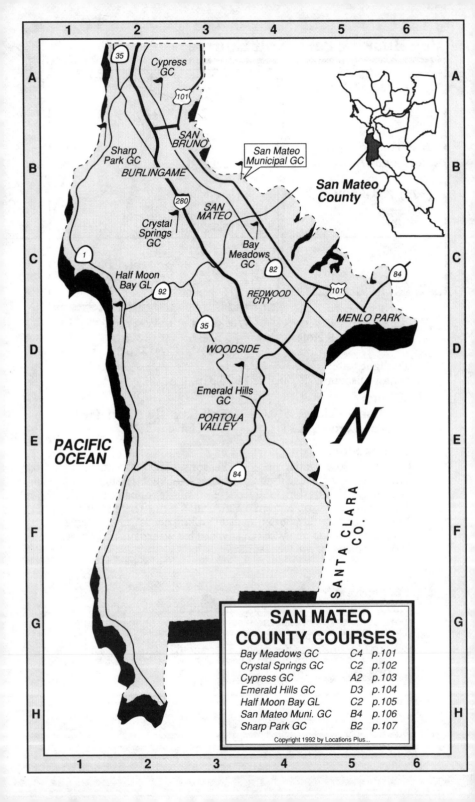

SAN MATEO COUNTY COURSES

Bay Meadows Golf Course

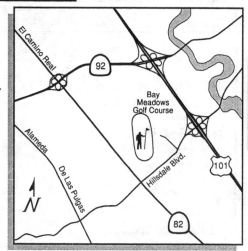

2600 South Delaware St.
San Mateo, CA 94402

(415) 341-7204

9 Hole Course

Green Fees:

	Weekdays	Weekends
9 Holes:	$6.00	$7.00
18 Holes:		

Twilight Rate: n.a.
Senior Discount: Weekdays only with play card

Outfitting:

Golf Car - 9 Holes: n.a.   Golf Car - 18 Holes: n.a.
Pull Carts: $2.00   Clubs: $3.00

Lessons & More:

Club Pro: n.a.   Lessons: n.a.
This course is open 7 days a week from the end of January through August. The remainder of the time, due to the races, they are only open Monday and Tuesday. They do have a Snack Bar for your convenience. They do not take reservations, first come, first served.

Facts & Figures:

This nine hole, par three course sits in the middle of the Bay Meadows Race Track. At first, it was just a driving range till about 15 years ago when they turned it into a Par 3 course which plays for a total of 1365 yards. The course is flat and easy to walk, ideal for beginners and seniors. There are 250 to 300 golfers a day out here at Bay Meadows during the months of May, June and July.

Crystal Springs Golf Club

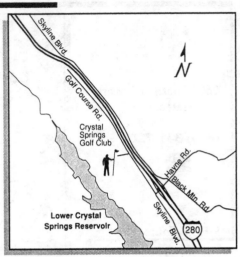

6650 Golf Course Drive
Burlingame, CA 94010

(415) 342-0603

18 Hole Course

Green Fees:

	Weekdays	Weekends
9 Holes:	n.a.	n.a.
18 Holes:	$38.00	$45.00
Twilight Rate: After 2:30	$29.00	$39.00
Senior Discount: n.a.		

Outfitting:

Golf Car - 9 Holes: $16.00	Golf Car - 18 Holes: *$22.00
Pull Carts: $3.00	Clubs: $15.00 + tax

Lessons & More:

Club Pro: Roger Graves   **Lessons:** $30 / 30 Minutes
A Practice Putting Green and Driving Range are available. Bucket
prices: $3.00 - $5.00. Their restaurant is open from 8 a.m. until 6
p.m., a lounge is also available. The Pro Shop carries a full line of
golf accessories. Weekday reservations can be made 7 days in
advance. Weekend reservations can be made on the prior
Monday after 6:00 a.m. *Golf Car rental is $11.00 per person
for 18 holes. Golf Cars mandatory on weekends.

Facts & Figures:

This course, designed by W. Herbert Fowler, opened in 1924.
It was later redesigned by Billy Bell, Jr. Course yardages and
ratings are: Championship 6683, 72.1; Regular 6,321, 70.7 and
Ladies' 5890, 74.0. Par for the course is 72. The course record of
63 is held by Charles Leider. Located on a watershed, this course
draws an abundance of wildlife, perhaps one or two Bobcats will
make an appearance at your golf outing.

102

Cypress Golf Course

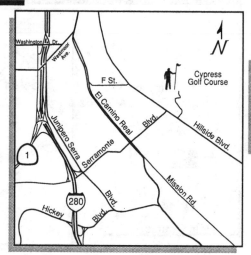

2001 Hillside Blvd.
Colma, CA 94014

(415) 992-5155

9 Hole Course

Green Fees:

	Weekdays	Weekends
9 Holes:	$10.00	$15.00
18 Holes:		

Twilight Rate: n.a.
Senior Discount: $7.00 before 9:00 a.m. Monday-Friday

Outfitting:

Golf Car - 9 Holes: $10.00	Golf Car - 18 Holes: $20.00
Pull Carts: $2.00	Clubs: n.a.

Lessons & More:

Club Pro: Don Giovannini   **Lessons:** $30 / 60 Minutes
Cypress Golf Course offers a Practice Putting Green, Chipping
Green and a Driving Range. Bucket prices: $4.00 - $6.00. Licata's
Restaurant and lounge are open for your convenience. The Pro
Shop carries a limited inventory of golf equipment. Reservations
can be made one week in advance. Their least busy days are
Mondays and Tuesdays.

Facts & Figures:

Cypress Golf Course, formerly known as Cypress Hills, was
developed in the early 1960's. It was originally a 9 hole, par 3
course, grew to 18 holes, and now is once again only a 9 hole
course. It boasts of being one of the longest 9 hole courses in
California measuring 3443 yards. There is only one par 3 hole,
two par 5 holes and the rest are par 4's. The longest par 5
measures 530 yards. Course par is 37, the record is 33. The hilly
terrain, tree lined fairways and a couple of water hazards help
flavor the course.

Emerald Hills Golf Course

San Mateo County

1059 Wilmington Way
Redwood City, CA 94062

(415) 368-7820

9 Hole Course

Green Fees:

	Weekdays	Weekends
9 Holes:	$6.00	$7.00
18 Holes:	$10.00	$12.00

Twilight Rate: n.a.
Senior Discount: $4.00 9 Holes, weekdays

Outfitting:

Golf Car - 9 Holes: n.a.	Golf Car - 18 Holes:
Pull Carts: n.a.	Clubs: $3.00

Lessons & More:

Club Pro: Bruce Olson   Lessons: Yes
There is a Practice Putting Green, a Chipping Green and a new
Driving cage available at Emerald Hills Golf Course. In the Pro
Shop you will find assorted beverages and snacks along with a
limited supply of golf accessories. They do not take reservations,
first come, first served. Elk Club members receive a discount on
Green Fees.

Facts & Figures:

Emerald Hills Golf Course belongs to the Elk's Lodge, but is still
open to the public. The course is short measuring 1163 yards
from the Men's Tees and 1138 yards from the Ladies' Tees.
Emerald Hills is well named for its location. This course will
present a challenge to most golfers because of its many trees and
narrow fairways. Bring along a fishing pole, if the golf is not
going well, try your luck in one of the three ponds you will find
on the course.

104

Half Moon Bay Golf Links

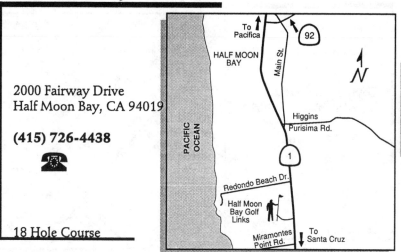

2000 Fairway Drive
Half Moon Bay, CA 94019

(415) 726-4438

18 Hole Course

Green Fees:

	Weekdays	Weekends
9 Holes:	n.a.	n.a.
18 Holes:	$65.00	$85.00
Twilight Rate: After 2/3 p.m.	$42.00	$47.00 Sunday
Senior Discount: n.a.		

Outfitting:

Golf Car - 9 Holes:	Golf Car - 18 Holes: Included
Pull Carts: n.a.	Clubs: $15.00

Lessons & More:

Club Pro: Moon Mullins   Lessons: $30 / 30 Minutes
A Practice Putting Green and Chipping Green are available at Half
Moon Bay Golf Links, but no Driving Range. Enterprize Saloon
Restaurant and Lounge is open from 7 a.m. until 8 p.m. for your
convenience. Their Pro Shop carries a full line of golf accesso-
ries. Reservations can be made 7 days in advance, Sat. for Sat.,
etc., beginning at day break. They offer a replay for $20.00. Golf
Cars are included in the Green Fees.

Facts & Figures:

Half Moon Bay Golf Links opened in October of 1973. Designer
of the course is Francis Duane with Arnold Palmer as a consult-
ant. The greens and fairways have been overhauled adding to the
playability of the course. The course rating is 74.5. Total
yardage from the Championship Tees is 7116. The Johnny
Walker Red Label Rock and Roll Golf Tournament is held here
annually. This challenging course has more then its fair share of
hazards, including barrancas.

San Mateo Municipal Golf Course

Coyote Point Drive
San Mateo, CA 94401

(415) 347-1461

18 Hole Course

Green Fees:

	Weekdays	Weekends
9 Holes:	n.a.	n.a.
18 Holes:	$14.00	$18.00

Twilight Rate: 9 Holes $9.50 after 2:00 p.m.
Senior Discount: $9.50 - San Mateo city residents

Outfitting:

Golf Car - 9 Holes:	Golf Car - 18 Holes: $18.00
Pull Carts: $2.00	Clubs: $8.50

Lessons & More:

Club Pro: Jake Montes   **Lessons:** $17.50 / 30 Minutes
There is a Practice Putting Green and a Chipping Green at San
Mateo Golf Course. The First Tee Restaurant is open from 6 a.m.
until 4:00 daily. There is a separate cocktail lounge. The Pro
Shop will be able to fill your golfing needs. Reservations can be
made seven days in advance. Their busiest days of the week are
Wednesdays through Sundays, the least busy day is Monday.

Facts & Figures:

This 18 hole course sits out on Coyote Point, subject to all the
breezes of the San Francisco Bay. The course is flat with narrow
fairways. There is a reservoir on hole #6 and a creek runs along
holes #3, 14, 16 and #17. There is a lake on hole #18. The course
from the Blue Tees is 5853 yards and is rated 66.5, from the
White Tees it is 5496 yards, rated 64.7 and from the Gold it is
5451 yards, rated 69.7. Par 70/72.

Sharp Park Golf Course

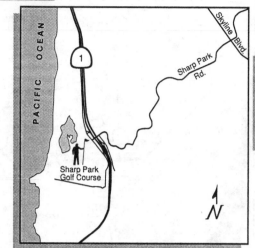

Highway 1
Pacifica, CA 94044

(415) 359-3380

18 Hole Course

Green Fees:

	Weekdays	Weekends
9 Holes:	*$8.00	*$10.00
18 Holes:	$15.00	$19.00

Twilight Rate: Same as 9 Hole Fees
Senior Discount: $7 Wkdys./$12 Wknds. with resident cards.

Outfitting:

Golf Car - 9 Holes: $10.00   Golf Car - 18 Holes: $18.00
      Pull Carts: $3.00   Clubs: $10 / $12

Lessons & More:

Club Pro: Jack R. Gage   **Lessons:** $30 / 30 Minutes
Sharp Park offers a Practice Putting Green and a Chipping Green.
They have a full restaurant serving from 6 a.m. until 10 p.m. The
Pro Shop carries a complete line of golf equipment. Reservations
for Saturday Tee Times can be made on Wednesdays prior, and
for Sunday Tee Times on Thursdays prior. Weekday reservations
can be made on Sundays. ***9 Hole rates available only on back
9 before 8:00 a.m.**

Facts & Figures:

This 18 hole links course is often referred to as "The Poor Man's
Pebble Beach". The back 9 holes run along the shore of the
Pacific Ocean providing the golfer with beautiful views as well as
an occasional stiff ocean breeze. The course is heavily treed, has
several water holes and the greens are fairly small. The course
was designed by Alister Mackenzie, and built by Jack Fleming in
1929. The course plays for a total of 6273 yards and is rated 70.0
from the Men's Tees, slope 115. The Ladies' rating is 73.0 and
slope is 120. Par for the course is 72, course record is 63 and held
by George Archer.

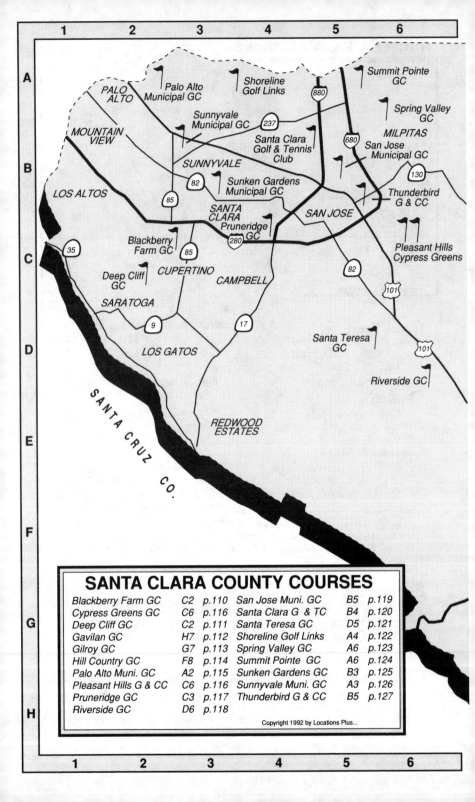

SANTA CLARA COUNTY COURSES

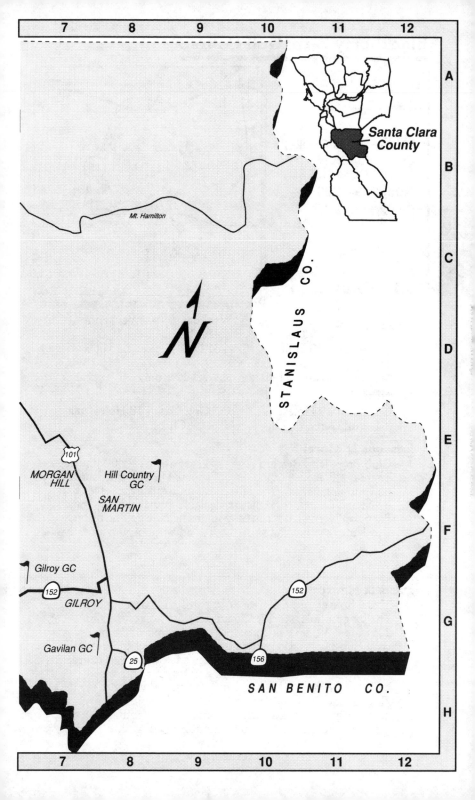

Blackberry Farm Golf Course

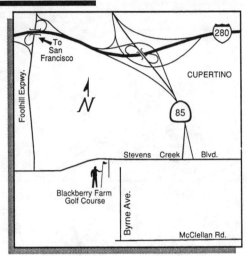

22100 Stevens Creek Bl.
Cupertino, CA 95014

(408) 253-9200

9 Hole Course

Green Fees:

	Weekdays	Weekends
9 Holes:	$6.75	$8.50
18 Holes:	$12.50	$15.00

Twilight Rate: n.a.
Senior Discount: $1.00 less on weekdays only

Outfitting:

Golf Cars - 9 Holes: n.a.	Golf Cars - 18 Holes: n.a.
Pull Carts: $2.00	Clubs: $4.50

Lessons & More:

Club Pro: Jeff Piserchio   Lessons: $32/ 40 Minutes
There is a Practice Putting Green, a netted hitting enclosure, but no Chipping Green. The Blue Pheasant Restaurant serves both lunch and dinner, cocktails are available in the lounge. Their Pro Shop is small, but can fill your immediate golfing needs. Tee Times can be made one week in advance beginning early morings.

Facts & Figures:

This 9 hole course plays for 1625 yards and has a par of 29. The longest hole, #2, is 292 yards, the 6th hole is the shortest at 101 yards. Water will come into play on four of the holes. A wise club selection is needed on the 3rd hole since it plays shorter due to the tee's elevation, the ball can easily clear the surrounding fence or ricochet off a nearby maintenance building. A high fence and a deep creek bed will shadow the 7th, 8th and 9th holes and may cause some golfers to over-compensate. This is a narrow course so any combination of hooks or slices can lead to a frustrating day of golf.

Deep Cliff Golf Course

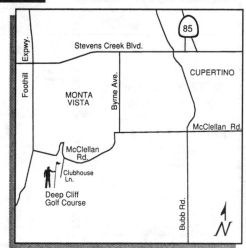

10700 Clubhouse Lane
Cupertino, CA 95014

(408) 253-5357

18 Hole Course

Green Fees:

	Weekdays	Weekends
9 Holes:	n.a.	n.a.
18 Holes:	$15.00	19.00
Twilight Rate:	$13.00	$17.00
Senior Discount:	n.a.	

Outfitting:

Golf Cars - 9 Holes: n.a.   Golf Cars - 18 Holes: n.a.
Pull Carts: $3.00   Clubs: $5.00 - $10.00

Lessons & More:

Club Pro: Lessons: n.a.
There is a Practice Putting Green, but no Driving Range at Deep Cliff Golf Course. The restaurant, Pro Shop and parking lot are new. The restaurant remains open from 7 a.m. until dusk. Reservations can be made seven days in advance by phone.

Facts & Figures:

This course opened for play in 1961. During 1989 many improvements were made to the course including rebuilding of the tees and greens. There are numerous elevated tees and rolling fairways lined by tall pine trees. A wandering creek and two ponds will come into play on more than half of the holes. This is a relatively short course at 3654 yards from the Men's Tees and 3424 from the Women's. Par 60. The longest hole is the 2nd at 327 yards, a par 4. The 17th hole is the shortest at 100 yards. Par 3's range from 100 to 186 yards. This is a course that will reward the finesse golfer.

Gavilan Golf Course

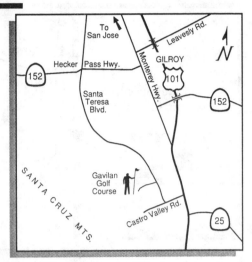

5055 Santa Teresa Blvd.
Gilroy, GC 95020

(408) 848-1363

9 Hole Course

Green Fees:

	Weekdays	Weekends
9 Holes:	$8.00	$10.00
18 Holes:	$8.00	$10.00
Twilight Rate: After 3 / 4 p.m.	$5.00	$5.00
Senior Discount: $6.00 Weekdays only		

Outfitting:

Golf Cars - 9 Holes: $10.00   Golf Cars - 18 Holes: $10.00
Pull Carts: $1.00   Clubs: $2.00

Lessons & More:

Club Pro: Lessons: n.a.
Gavilan Golf Course offers a Practice Putting Green, Chipping
Green and a Driving Range. Bucket prices: $1.00 - $3.00. This
is a nine hole course with the tees offset to change the dis-
tances and angles for the back nine. Snacks and beverages are
available along with a number of golf accessories at the Pro
Shop. They do not take reservations.

Facts & Figures:

The course opened in 1968 and abuts Gavilan College. This is
a short course at only 3638 yards from both the Men's and
Women's Tees. Pars are 62 for the men and 63 for the women.
Although the course is short the distance seems greater if
you're walking due to the rolling terrain. This is especially true
on the 2nd and 9th holes. An out-of-bounds fence and road-
way shadows the 3rd hole on the right side. Water comes into
play only on the 8th hole, a deceptively short par 3, 87 yards.
The holes will range in length from the 8th at 87 yards to the
3rd at 356 yards.

Gilroy Golf Course

2695 Hecker Pass Hwy.
Gilroy, CA 95020

(408) 842-2501

9 Hole Course

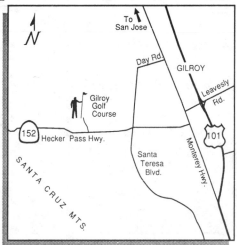

Green Fees:

	Weekdays	Weekends
9 Holes:	$12.00	$16.00
18 Holes:	$12.00	$16.00
Twilight Rate:	$9.00	$10.00
Senior Discount: Yes		

Outfitting:

Golf Cars - 9 Holes: $10.00	Golf Cars - 18 Holes: $20.00
Pull Carts: $2.00	Clubs: $6.00

Lessons & More:

Club Pro: Don DeLorenzo   **Lessons:** $20 / 30 Minutes
A Driving Range, Chipping Green and Practice Putting Green
are available at Gilroy. The Gilroy Golf Course Restaurant is
open from 10 a.m. until 3 p.m. The Pro Shop carries a full line
of golf equipment. Reservations can be made seven days in
advance. Their busiest day of the week is Friday, least busy on
Thursday.

Facts & Figures:

The course was opened in the early 1920's and hosts the
"Gilroy Garlic Festival Golf Tournament" and the "Special
Olympics Tournament". This is a 9 hole course with separate
tee placements when playing 18. If you are going around twice
you may find it plays longer than the 5798 yards from the
Men's Tees or 5501 from the Women's, due to a number of
fairways hugging the hillsides. Course par is 70/72. Course
record is held by George Archer with a 61. There are areas on
this course where you will be hitting the ball from a blind spot.
You need to be a good judge of distance to score well on these
tough holes.

113

Hill Country Golf Course

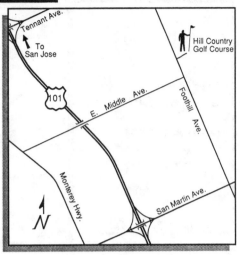

15060 Foothill Avenue
Morgan Hill, CA 95037

(408) 779-4136

18 Hole Course

Green Fees:

	Weekdays	Weekends
9 Holes:	n.a.	n.a.
18 Holes:	$10.00	$12.00

Twilight Rate: n.a.
Senior Discount: Less $2.00

Outfitting:

Golf Cars - 9 Holes:	Golf Cars - 18 Holes: $12.00
Pull Carts: $3.00	Clubs: n.a.

Lessons & More:

Club Pro: Jan Perch   Lessons: *$25 / 30 Minutes
Hill Country Golf Course is closed on Mondays. Their warm-up facility is a Practice Putting Green. The Flying Lady Restaurant is open from 12:00 noon to 2:30 p.m. and 5:00 p.m. to 8:30 p.m. on Wed. thru Sun; closed on Mon. and Tues. Cocktails are available in the lounge. There is a Pro Shop for your convenience. Reservations can be made at anytime. *George Ekberg is the teaching pro.

Facts & Figures:

If you enjoy the challenge of water hazards you will enjoy this course. On ten of the holes water comes into play, on six of the holes you will need to traverse water to approach the greens. This is a short, par 58, course. From the Men's Tees the distance is 3110 yards and from the Women's only 2753 yards. There are four par 4 holes and the remaining are par 3's. The longest hole is #1, par 4, at 368 yards, with the 7th hole being the shortest at 98 yards. This course offers an abundance of work for those irons.

Palo Alto Municipal Golf Course

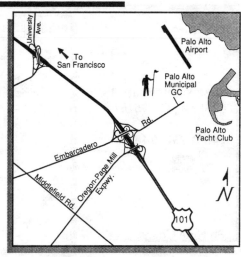

1875 Embarcadero Road
Palo Alto, CA 94303

(415) 856-0881

18 Hole Course

Santa Clara County

Green Fees:

	Weekdays	Weekends
9 Holes:	*$9.00	*$10.00
18 Holes:	$14.00	$18.00
Twilight Rate:	$9.00	$12.00

Senior Discount: $11.00, wkdys / Palo Alto residents only.

Outfitting:

Golf Cars - 9 Holes:	Golf Cars - 18 Holes: $17.00
Pull Carts: $3.00	Clubs: $12.50

Lessons & More:

Club Pro: Brad Lozares   Lessons: $30 / 30 Minutes
This course offers a Practice Putting Green and a Driving
Range. Bucket prices: $2.00 - $4.75. Harry's Hofbrau is open 7
a.m. to 6 p.m. Brad Lozares' Golf Shop is complete. Weekend
reservations can be made on the Tuesday prior beginning at
7:00 a.m. and 7 days in advance for weekdays. They are least
busy Mon. thru Thur. after 1:00. **9 Hole Fees apply the 1st
1/2 hour from back 9.**

Facts & Figures:

The course opened in 1956 and has been redesigned by Robert
Trent Jones, Jr. The course is a long par 72 for the men and 73
for the women. Yardage from the Men's Tees is 6525 and from
the Women's 5852 yards. If you are playing from the Pro Tees
the distance is 6854 yards. This is a pretty straight, flat course,
with only one water hazard. The holes will range from a long
521 yards, par 5, on #1 to a short 149 yards, par 3, on #3. The
course record of 64 is held by Brad Heninger. Their putting
greens are among the best in the area for a public course.

115

Pleasant Hills & Cypress Greens

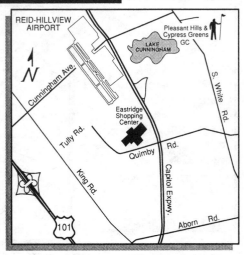

2050 South White Road
San Jose, CA 95151

(408) 238-3485

36 Hole Course

Green Fees:

	Weekdays	Weekends
9 Holes:	n.a.	n.a.
18 Holes:	$17.00	$22.00
Twilight Rate: After 2:00 p.m	$11.00	$13.00
Senior Discount: $11.00 all day, weekdays only		

Outfitting:

Golf Cars - 9 Holes: $11.00	Golf Cars - 18 Holes: $19.00
Pull Carts: $2.50	Clubs: $10.00

Lessons & More:

Club Pro: n.a.   Lessons: n.a.

Pleasant Hills Golf & Country Club offers a Practice Putting Green and a Chipping Green, but no Driving Range. Their clubhouse serves a variety of food and beverages. The Pro Shop carries a limited amount of golf equipment. Reservations can be made one week in advance. **Cypress Greens Golf Course Green Fees are $7.00 on weekdays and $9.00 on weekends. No Twilight Rate or Senior Discount available.**

Facts & Figures:

Pleasant Hills Golf and Country Club and Cypress Greens have shared this location for the past 30 years. Pleasant Hills is a fairly long course measuring 6888 yards from the Blue Tees, 6519 from the White and 6084 from the Red Tees. Par is 72 / 75. The fairways are wide and lined with numerous older trees that have recently been trimmed. No other renovations in the last several years. Cypress Greens is an 18 hole, par 3 course that plays for a total of 2631 yards. These courses are set back far enough from the major roads to give a feeling of seclusion.

Pruneridge Golf Club

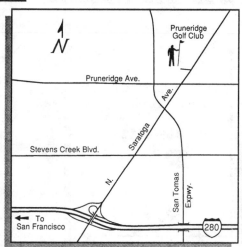

400 North Saratoga Ave.
Santa Clara, CA 95050

(408) 248-4424

9 Hole Course

Green Fees:

	Weekdays	Weekends
9 Holes:	$8.00	$9.50
18 Holes:	$16.00	$19.00

Twilight Rate: n.a.
Senior Discount: $7.00 with Membership

Outfitting:

Golf Cars - 9 Holes: n.a.	Golf Cars - 18 Holes: n.a.
Pull Carts: $1.50	Clubs: $5.00

Lessons & More:

Club Pro: Wyane Wallick   **Lessons:** $30 / 45 Minutes
A Practice Putting Green and Driving Range are available at Pruneridge. Bucket price: $2.25 / 30 balls. The Pro Shop carries a large selection of golf accessories. There is also a Snack Bar open from dawn to dusk featuring deli-type sandwiches and beverages. Reservations are taken one week in advance beginning at daybreak.

Facts & Figures:

The course was built on the site of a former prune orchard in 1964 by Charlie & Betty Lester Boyd. At that time the course was known as "Pruneridge Farms Golf Course". The course was sold in 1977 and the new owner changed the name to "Pruneridge Golf Club". Remodeling of the course was completed in 1978 with the help of Robert Trent Jones, Jr. This 9 hole course is 1860 yards in length and includes five par 3's and four par 4's. Course rating for 18 holes is 56.3, slope 73. This course continues to upgrade their facilities. It is in good shape for being so heavily played.

Riverside Golf Course

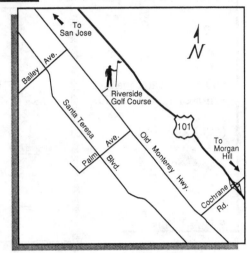

Old Monterey Highway
Coyote, CA 95013

(408) 463-0622

18 Hole Course

Green Fees:

	Weekdays	Weekends
9 Holes:	n.a.	n.a.
18 Holes:	$19.00	$25.00
Twilight Rate:	$15.00	$19.00

Senior Discount: $15.00, weekdays only

Outfitting:

Golf Cars - 9 Holes: $16.00	Golf Cars - 18 Holes: $24.00
Pull Carts: $5.00	Clubs: $10.00

Lessons & More:

Club Pro: Tom Smith   Lessons: $30 / 30 Minutes
A Practice Putting Green and a Driving Range are available at
Riverside. The Pro Shop carries a full line of merchandise. The
Riverside Restaurant is open from 8 a.m. until 4 p.m. serving
snacks and beverages. Reservations can be made starting at
12:00 noon on Saturday for the following Saturday & Sunday
and one week in advance for weekdays.

Facts & Figures:

This well maintained championship course opened in 1957.
The course is rated 71 from the Blue Tees and 69 from the
White Tees. Yardage 6825 and 6504 respectively, Par 72. The
official course record is a 67 with an unsanctioned course
record of 63. The course hosts a number of tournaments each
year which include the "American Cancer Society" and "The
Mark Winters Leukemia Memorial". The course is south of San
Jose and situated between Highway 101 on the east and Old
Monterey Highway on the west. The entrance is from Old
Monterey Highway between Palm and Bailey Avenues.

San Jose Municipal Golf Course

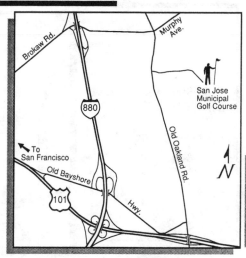

1560 Old Oakland Road
San Jose, CA 95131

(408) 441-4653

18 Hole Course

Green Fees:

	Weekdays	Weekends
9 Holes:	*$12.00	*$15.00
18 Holes:	$20.00	$27.00
Twilight Rate: After 2 / 3 p.m.	$12.00	$15.00
Senior Discount: $12.00 wkdys. with San Jose resident card		

Outfitting:

Golf Cars - 9 Holes: $11.00	Golf Cars - 18 Holes: $20.00
Pull Carts: $2..50	Clubs: $10.00

Lessons & More:

Club Pro: Mike Rawitser   Lessons: Yes
San Jose Municipal has a Practice Putting Green, Chipping
Green and a Driving Range. Bucket prices: $2.00 - $5.00. A
Pro Shop, restaurant and lounge will fill most golfers' require-
ments. Weekend reservations are taken on the prior Tuesday at
7:00 a.m. and one week in advance for weekdays. *The first
hour of the day from back 9.

Facts & Figures:

San Jose Municipal is a long course at 6401 yards from the
Men's Tees, 5484 yards from the Women's and 6916 from the
Pro's. Bunkers will come into play on nearly every hole, most
commonly near the greens. The length on some of the par 3's
will pose difficulty in club selection. For example, the 17th
hole is a par 3 at 170 yards and a difficult play over water with
two traps skirting the green. The proper club selection will
make a tremendous difference on this hole. San Jose Municipal
also serves as home to a number of Prairie Owls, it can make
searching for that hooked ball an interesting wildlife outing.

Santa Clara Golf & Tennis Club

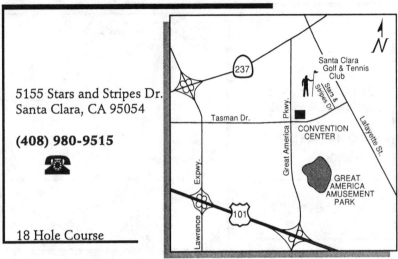

5155 Stars and Stripes Dr.
Santa Clara, CA 95054

(408) 980-9515

18 Hole Course

Green Fees:

	Weekdays	Weekends
9 Holes:	n.a.	n.a.
18 Holes:	$16.00	$22.00
Twilight Rate:	$10.00	$14.00
Senior Discount:	$60.00 per month weekdays only	

Outfitting:

Golf Cars - 9 Holes: $9.00	Golf Cars - 18 Holes: $18.00
Pull Carts: $2.00	Clubs: $10.00

Lessons & More:

Club Pro: Tom Hale   **Lessons:** $40 / Lesson
Santa Clara Golf and Tennis Club offers a Practice Putting
Green, a Chipping Green and a Driving Range. Bucket prices:
$2.50 - $5.00. David's Restaurant is open from 6 a.m. until 11
p.m. A cocktail lounge and complete Pro Shop are available for
your convenience. Reservations can be made 7 days in advance starting at 7:00 a.m.

Facts & Figures:

Santa Clara Golf and Tennis Club opened on April 5, 1987,
adjacent to the Santa Clara Convention Center. This is a very
busy course with over 400 tournaments being played here each
year. The course measures 6822 yards from the Blue Tees,
6457 yards from the White and 5639 yards from the Red Tees.
The ratings are 72.2, 70.5 and 66.6, respectively. The course
record is 66 from the Men's Tees and 67 from the Women's.
This course is somewhat exposed to winds by being in the
valley with few windbreaks available. This can add an interesting dimension to judging the strength of your golf swing.

Santa Teresa Golf Club

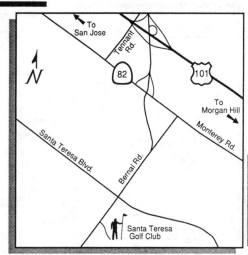

260 Bernal Road
San Jose, CA 95119

(408) 225-2650

18 Hole Course

Green Fees:

	Weekdays	Weekends
9 Holes:	*$13.00	*$16.00
18 Holes:	$22.00	$30.00

Twilight Rate: Same as 9 hole fees
Senior Discount: $13 Wkdys./Before 10 am, between 1&2 pm

Outfitting:

Golf Cars - 9 Holes: $11.00   Golf Cars - 18 Holes: $20.00
Pull Carts: $3.00   Clubs: $ 8.00 / $12.00

Lessons & More:

Club Pro: Bob Mejias   **Lessons:** Variable Rate
Santa Teresa has a Practice Putting Green, Chipping Green and a Driving Range. Bucket prices: $3.00 - $5.00. Their Bar and Grill is open from 6 a.m. until 10 p.m. The Pro Shop carries a complete line of merchandise. Reservations can be made starting at 8:00 a.m. on Monday for the following Saturday & Sunday. Weekday reservations can be made 7 days in advance at 6 a.m. * 9 Hole Fees apply for 1st hour in a.m.

Facts & Figures:

The course opened in 1962. A new clubhouse was completed in 1987. The course is a long 6742 yards from the Championship Tees with a par of 71. From the regular tees the yardage comes down from 6430 with the Women's yardage at 6027. The course record of 64 is held by John Snopkowski. The hole selection has three par 5's at 492, 479 and a whopping 529 yards. Even the four par 3's play long with an average length of 168.5 yards. There are doglegs galore, some having very challenging angles. If you are walking the course it will seem longer than the 3.65 miles due to the rolling landscape.

121

Shoreline Golf Links

2600 N. Shoreline Blvd.
Mountain View, CA
94043

(415) 969-2041

18 Hole Course

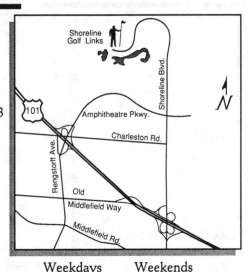

Green Fees:

	Weekdays	Weekends
9 Holes:	*$17.00	*$17.00
18 Holes:	$29.00	$38.00

Twilight Rate: After 1:00 / 4:00 p.m. same as 9 hole fees
Senior Discount: $21.00 weekdays only

Outfitting:

Golf Cars - 9 Holes: $10.00	Golf Cars - 18 Holes: $20.00
Pull Carts: $2.50	Clubs: $12.00

Lessons & More:

Club Pro: Teaching Pro's   **Lessons:** $40 / 60Minutes
A Practice Putting Green, Chipping Green and Driving Range
are all available at Shoreline Golf Links. The Snack Bar is open
from dawn to dusk. The Pro Shop carries a complete line of
golf accessories. Weekend reservations can be made on the
Monday prior at 7:00, weekdays reservations can be made 7
days in advance. ***1st 1 1/2 hr. in a.m. from back 9.**

Facts & Figures:

Shoreline Golf Links, originally known as "Shoreline Golf
Course", opened in 1983. Located in Mountain View's
Shoreline Regional Park, the course has both a proximity to the
Bay as well as a gently rolling terrain that is typical of a tradi-
tional Scottish style links course. Remodeling of the course, by
Robert Trent Jones, Jr., in 1986-1987 brought the similarity
closer.   Course par is 72 and the length is a healthy 6819 yards
from the Pro Tees, 6235 yards from the Men's and 5488 yards
from the Women's. Chien Soon Lu holds the course record of
64.

Spring Valley Golf Course

3441 East Calaveras Blvd.
Milpitas, CA 95035

(408) 262-1722

18 Hole Course

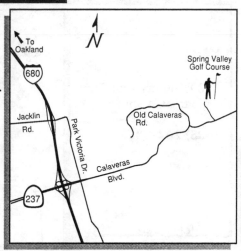

Green Fees:

	Weekdays	Weekends
9 Holes:	*$12.00	*$15.00
18 Holes:	$18.00	$26.00
Twilight Rate:	$13.00	$15.00
Senior Discount:	$14.00 weekdays only	

Outfitting:

Golf Cars - 9 Holes:	Golf Cars - 18 Holes: $20.00
Pull Carts: $2.00	Clubs: $15.00

Lessons & More:

Club Pro: R. Stewart/D. Jetter   **Lessons:** $45 / 30 Minutes
Spring Valley offers both a Practice Putting Green and a Driving
Range. Bucket price: $3.00. Their restaurant is open from 8
a.m. until 3 p.m. weekdays and 6 a.m. until 3 p.m. on weekends. A lounge and Pro Shop are also available. Weekend
reservations can be made one week in advance in person or on
Monday by calling. Their busiest day is Friday, least busy day
is Monday. ***Back 9 holes only in early a.m.**

Facts & Figures:

The Spring Valley Golf Course opened in 1956. The length of
the course is moderate at 6099 yards, pars 70 / 73. The holes
range in length from a par 5, 510 yards on #6, down to a pair of
150 yard, par 3's, on #2 and #7. To add a bit of a challenge, on
three of the holes you tee off directly facing water. It is a
predominantly straight course with the exception of mild
doglegs, the most difficult being on the 10th at an approximate
45 degree angle. They have recently finished rebuilding several
tees and greens as well as an entire hole.

123

Summit Pointe Golf Club

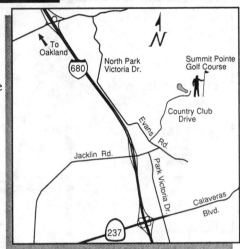

1200 Country Club Drive
Milpitas, CA 95035

(408) 262-8813

18 Hole Course

Green Fees:

	Weekdays	Weekends
9 Holes:	n.a.	n.a.
18 Holes:	*$20.00	*$31.00

Twilight Rate: $10 at 3 p.m., $15 at 1 p.m.
Senior Discount: $15.00 during the week.

Outfitting:

Golf Cars - 9 Holes: Golf Cars - 18 Holes: $20.00
    Pull Carts: $2.00   Clubs: $10.00

Lessons & More:

Club Pro: Mark Dorcak   **Lessons:** $30 / 45 Minutes
Summit Pointe has both a Practice Putting Green and a Driving
Range. The Club at Summit Pointe is open from 7 a.m. until 9
p.m. The Pro Shop is complete. Weekend reservations can be
made on the Saturday prior beginning at 7:00 a.m. and for
weekdays seven days in advance. *Weekdays: $30 w/cart per
person, Weekends: $40 w/cart per person.

Facts & Figures:

Summit Pointe opened on August 19, 1978 as "Tularcitos Golf
Course". It became Summit Pointe in 1988 after changing
hands. The entire course was renovated in 1988-1989 including the cart paths and clubhouse. The course has a par of 72
and averages 6000 yards in length. From the Pro Tees the
yardage is 6311, from the Men's 6048 and from the Women's
5496. The course record of 65 is held by Estaban Toledo. The
course regularly hosts the "Milpitas/Berryessa YMCA" Tournament.

Sunken Gardens Municipal Golf Course

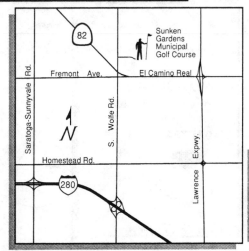

1010 South Wolfe Road
Sunnyvale, CA 94086

(408) 739-6588

9 Hole Course

Green Fees:

	Weekdays	Weekends
9 Holes:	$7.00	$9.00
18 Holes:	$11.50	$15.00

Twilight Rate: Yes
Senior Discount: Sunnyvale residents only

Outfitting:

Golf Cars - 9 Holes: n.a.*	Golf Cars - 18 Holes: n.a.*
Pull Carts: $2.00	Clubs: $4.00

Lessons & More:

Club Pro: Art Wilson   Lessons: $30 / Lesson
There is a Practice Putting Green and a Driving Range available.
Bucket prices: $3.00 - $5.00. Their restaurant is open from 6:30
a.m. until 3:00 p.m. Drinks are available in the lounge. The
Pro Shop is complete. Weekend reservations taken on the
Monday prior if resident of Sunnyvale, otherwise on Tuesday
prior. *A Golf Car is available for handicapped persons.

Facts & Figures:

The course plays for 1586 yards and has a par of 29. It is
nestled in a low-lying region that belies the fact it sits in the
midst of several congested roadways. The fairways are narrow
and bordered by many obstacles. Well executed iron shots are
the hallmark for a successful outing. The par 3's on #3 and #4
appear longer than they are so be careful in choosing your club.
The tee shot on #5 is a blind shot to the flag due to a large
cluster of trees. Water does not play a significant role, but due
to the strategic placement of several sand traps errant shots to
the greens can become most unpleasant.

Sunnyvale Municipal Golf Course

605 Macara Lane
Sunnyvale, CA 94086

(408) 738-3666

18 Hole Course

Green Fees:

	Weekdays	Weekends
9 Holes:	n.a.	n.a.
18 Holes:	$16.00	$21.00
Twilight Rate: After 2 p.m.	$11.00	$14.00

Senior Discount: Sunnyvale residents only

Outfitting:

Golf Cars - 9 Holes:	Golf Cars - 18 Holes: $19.00
Pull Carts: $3.00	Clubs: $10.00

Lessons & More:

Club Pro: Art Wilson   **Lessons:** $30 / 30 Minutes
The course offers a Practice Putting Green, but no Driving Range. The Lookout Inn Restaurant is open from 7 a.m. until 8 p.m. Art Wilson's Pro Shop carries a full line of golf merchandise. Weekend reservations can be made by Sunnyvale residents on the Monday prior starting at 6:00 a.m. and non-residents on Tuesday prior starting at 7:00 a.m. No weekday reservations taken, first come, first served.

Facts & Figures:

The Sunnyvale Municipal Golf Course has been open for nineteen years. Six of the holes were renovated in 1988. The course is 5744 yards from the Men's Tees and 5176 yards from the Women's Tees, with pars of 70 and 71, respectively. The 1st and the 5th holes will challenge you with doglegs approaching 90 degrees. The 8th green is delicately situated with water and traps on the perimeter. Water hazards need to be negotiated on 8 of the holes. The course plays hosts to many tournaments, including the Sunnyvale Service & Athletic Club.

Thunderbird Golf & Country Club

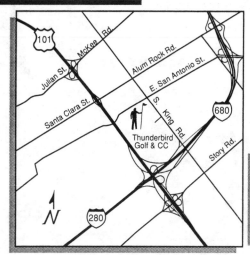

221 South King Road
San Jose, CA 95135

(408) 259-3355

18 Hole Course

Green Fees:

		Weekdays	Weekends
9 Holes:		n.a	n.a.
18 Holes:		$14.00	$17.00
Twilight Rate:	After 2 p.m.	$11.00	$14.00
Senior Discount:	$12.00 weekdays		

Outfitting:

Golf Cars - 9 Holes:	Golf Cars - 18 Holes: $15.00
Pull Carts: $2.00	Clubs: $4.00

Lessons & More:

Club Pro: Brigid Moreton   Lessons: Yes
There is a Practice Putting Green and a Driving Range at Thunderbird Golf and Country Club. Bucket prices range from $3.00 - $5.00. Only packaged snacks available. They do not take reservations, first come, first served.

Facts & Figures:

This public, 18 hole course is not considered long at 4802 yards, but it does have two par 5 holes at 450 yards each, and a par 4, 430 yard hole. Par for the course is a 64 for Men and a 65 for Women. The course has a rating of 58. Water will come into play on the 1st and the 9th holes, and except for slight doglegs on the 16th and 18th, the course is predominantly straight. Thunderbird Golf and Country Club is the sister to the Pleasant Hill Golf Course.

127

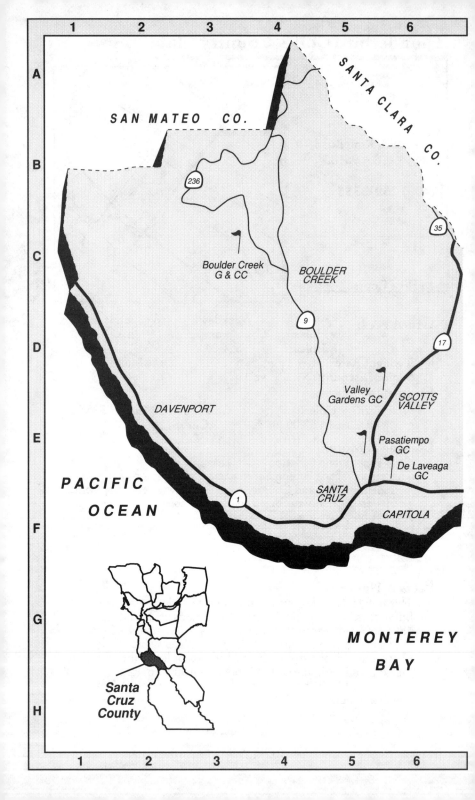

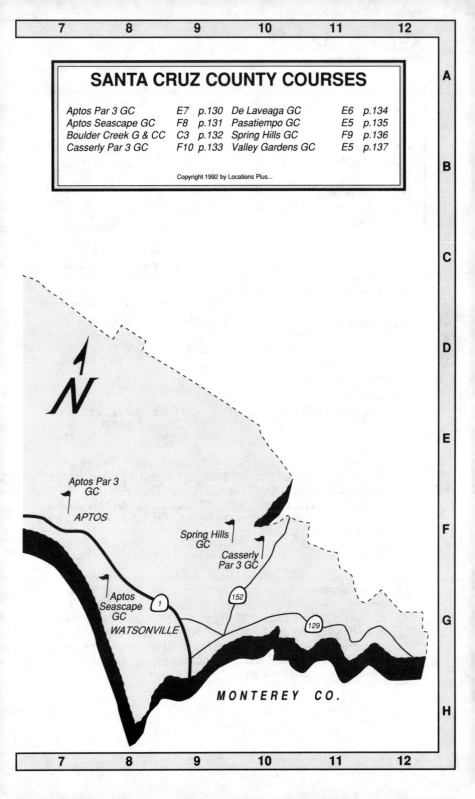

SANTA CRUZ COUNTY COURSES

Aptos Par 3

2600 Mar Vista Drive
Aptos, CA 95003

(408) 688-5000

9 Hole Course

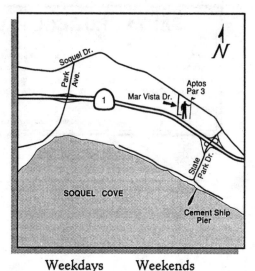

Green Fees:

	Weekdays	Weekends
9 Holes:	$5.00	$5.00
18 Holes:	$7.00	$8.00

Twilight Rate: n.a.
Senior Discount: n.a.

Outfitting:

Golf Cars - 9 Holes: n.a.	Golf Cars - 18 Holes:
Pull Carts: $1.00	Clubs: $4.00

Lessons & More:

Club Pro: Howard Menge **Lessons:** $20 / 30 Minutes
Aptos Par 3 offers a Practice Putting Green and a Driving Range,
Large Bucket: $3.00, Small Bucket: $2.00. Their Pro Shop special-
izes in custom made golf clubs. A Snack Bar is available only on
the weekends. Reservations can be made at any time. Their least
busy day is Monday.

Facts & Figures:

Aptos Par 3 golf course has been in operation since 1962. The
course plays for a total of 1068 yards. The holes range from a
short 85 yards on the 4th hole to 150 yards on the 8th hole. The
course record stands at 22. This is a tricky course, by no means
easy. Aptos Par 3 will test your short iron game as well as
provide a pleasurable walk.

Aptos Seascape Golf Course

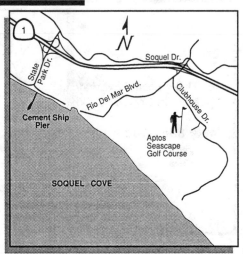

610 Clubhouse Drive
Aptos, CA 95003

(408) 688-3213

18 Hole Course

Green Fees:

	Weekdays	Weekends
9 Holes:	n.a.	n.a.
18 Holes:	$25.00	$42.00
Twilight Rate:	$20.00	$30.00
Senior Discount: n.a.		

Outfitting:

Golf Cars - 9 Holes:	Golf Cars - 18 Holes: $22.00
Pull Carts: $3.00	Clubs: $15.00

Lessons & More:

Club Pro: Don Elser   **Lessons:** $30 / 30 Minutes
This course offers 2 Practice Putting Greens, a Chipping Green
and a Driving Range. Bucket prices: $2.25 - $4.50. They have a
full restaurant and a Snack Bar available for your convenience.
Weekend reservations can be made on the Monday prior,
beginning at 10:00 a.m. and for weekday play, 7 days in advance
beginning at 7:30 a.m. Their busiest day is Friday their least busy
day is Tuesday.

Facts & Figures:

Aptos Seascape Golf Course originally opened as a 9 hole course
in 1926 and was known as Rio Del Mar Country Club. It was
expanded to 18 holes late in 1929. The course changed names
two more times before 1986 when it was purchased by the
American Golf Corporation. They renovated the pro shop and
restaurant and installed a fully automatic irrigation system on the
course. This is a beautiful course, tree lined, with rolling fairways. Total Men's yardage is 6123, and Women's yardage is
5656. Overall par is 72.

Boulder Creek Golf & Country Club

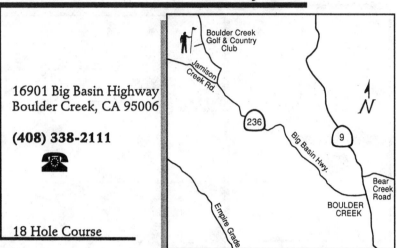

16901 Big Basin Highway
Boulder Creek, CA 95006

(408) 338-2111

18 Hole Course

Green Fees:

	Weekdays	Weekends
9 Holes:	n.a.	n.a.
18 Holes:	$16.00	$26.00
Twilight Rate:	$12.00	$16.00

Senior Discount: $11.00 Monday through Friday

Outfitting:

Golf Cars - 9 Holes: n.a. Golf Cars - 18 Holes: $16.00
Pull Carts: n.a. Clubs: $8.00

Lessons & More:

Club Pro: Hal Wells **Lessons:** $30 / Lesson
Boulder Creek has 2 Practice Putting Greens and a Chipping
Green, but no Driving Range. A full service Pro Shop is open for
your convenience. The Redwood Room is open for breakfast,
lunch and dinner. All reservations can be made seven days in
advance.

Facts & Figures:

Boulder Creek, designed by Jack Fleming, opened with 9 holes in
1961 and 9 more were added in 1966. It winds its way around
homes and condominiums and insists on the golfers being pretty
much on target. The course has been steadily improved, the
greens are great and it is a pleasure to play. Men's and Women's
course ratings are 61.3. Total yardage for the Men is 4279, par is
65, Women's yardage is 3970, par 65.

Casserly Par 3 Golf Course

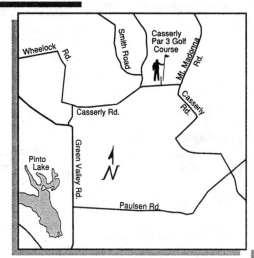

626 Casserly Road
Watsonville, CA 95076

(408) 724-1654

9 Hole Course

Green Fees:

	Weekdays	Weekends
9 Holes:	$4.00	$4.00
18 Holes:	$8.00	$8.00

Twilight Rate: n.a.
Senior Discount: n.a.

Outfitting:

Golf Cars - 9 Holes: n.a. Golf Cars - 18 Holes: n.a.
Pull Carts: $ .50 Clubs: $3.00

Lessons & More:

Club Pro: n.a. Lessons: n.a.

Casserly Par 3 Golf Course has a Practice Putting Green, but no Chipping Green or Driving Range. Their Pro Shop carries a limited amount of golf accessories. Candy bars and other such snacks are available along with soft beverages. Reservations are not taken, first come, first served.

Facts & Figures:

Casserly Par 3 Golf Course opened in 1966. This course has a second set of tees for playing a second nine holes. Total yardage for 18 holes is 2422, par 54. The longest hole would be #15, which is a straight shot to the green. There are two water holes, one on #6 in the middle of the fairway and the other on #5 just right of the green. The course record for playing 9 holes is 22 from the front tees, and 23 from the back tees.

De Laveaga Golf Course

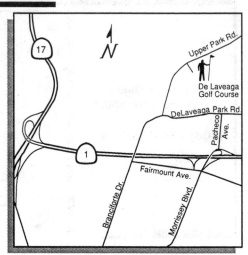

401 Upper Park Road
Santa Cruz, CA 95065

(408) 423-7212
☎

18 Hole Course

Green Fees:

	Weekdays	Weekends
9 Holes:	$13.00	$18.00
18 Holes:	$18.50	$25.00
Twilight Rate:	$12.00	$16.50

Senior Discount: County residents

Outfitting:

Golf Cars - 9 Holes: $13.00	Golf Cars - 18 Holes: $22.00
Pull Carts: $3.00	Clubs: $15.00

Lessons & More:

Club Pro: Gary Loustalot   **Lessons:** *$35 / 30 Minutes
This course offers a Practice Putting Green and a Driving Range.
Buckets range from $3 to $5. Full Clubhouse facilities are
available from 7 a.m. to 2:30 p.m. and the Snack Bar is open from
7 to 4. Reservations for weekdays can be made on the Sunday
prior at 2:00 p.m. and for the weekends on the Monday prior
beginning at 7:00 a.m. *Tom Rudy is the Teaching Professional.

Facts & Figures:

This difficult 18 hole course winds its way through the lovely
Santa Cruz Mountains. Every one of the 6010 yards is a challenge. There is no questioning the out-of-bounds markers on
these fairways that in many cases are set by steep, wooded
ravines. Out-of-bounds, in many cases, will result in lost balls.
If you enjoy a mountain outing you will definitely enjoy De
Laveaga. Par for the course is 72. The Men's rating is 70.1, slope
130, Ladies is 70.7, slope 126.

Pasatiempo Golf Course

18 Clubhouse Road
Santa Cruz, CA 95060

(408) 459-9155

18 Hole Course

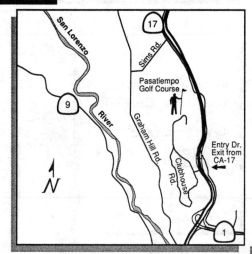

Green Fees:

	Weekdays	Weekends
9 Holes:	n.a.	n.a.
18 Holes:	$70.00	*$80.00
Twilight Rate: After 2 p.m.	$33.00	$39.00
Senior Discount: n.a.		

Outfitting:

Golf Cars - 9 Holes: $18.00	Golf Cars - 18 Holes: $27.00
Pull Carts: $5.00	Clubs: $20.00

Lessons & More:

Club Pro: Shawn McEntee   **Lessons:** $30 / 30 Minutes
Pasatiempo Golf Club offers a Practice Putting Green, Chipping
Green and a Driving Range. Bucket prices: $2.00 - $4.00. They
have a beautiful new Clubhouse and restaurant. The Pro Shop
carries a complete line of golf accessories. Weekend reservations
can be made on the Monday prior beginning at 10:00 a.m. and
weekday reservations can be made seven days in advance.
*Fridays Green Fees are the same as weekend fees.

Facts & Figures:

Marion Hollins, a U.S. Women's Amateur Champion, purchased
the 600 rolling acres near Monterey Bay and commissioned Dr.
Alister Mackenzie, a golf course architect from Scotland, to
design Pasatiempo which was completed in 1929. This championship course hosts the Western Intercollegiate Tournament each
spring and it has done so for the past 40 years. The ratings and
slopes are: Championship 72.9/138, Regular 71.4/134 and Ladies
72.9/133. A trip to Pasatiempo for a round of golf should prove
to be most enjoyable.

Spring Hills Golf Course

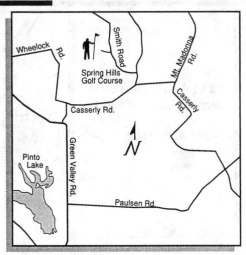

31 Smith Road
Watsonville, CA 95076

(408) 724-1404

18 Hole Course

Green Fees:

	Weekdays	Weekends
9 Holes:	n.a.	n.a.
18 Holes:	$15.00	$20.00
Twilight Rate:	$10.00	n.a.
Senior Discount: n.a.		

Outfitting:

Golf Cars - 9 Holes: $10.00   Golf Cars - 18 Holes: $20.00
Pull Carts: $2.00 / $3.00   Clubs: n.a.

Lessons & More:

Club Pro: n.a.   Lessons: Yes
This course offers a Practice Putting Green, Chipping Green and a
Driving Range. Medium Bucket: $2.50. Their Snack Bar is open
from 8 a.m. until 5 p.m. The Pro Shop carries the standard
necessities. Lessons are by appointment only. Reservations are
taken at anytime.

Facts & Figures:

Spring Hills Golf Course opened in 1965 and has steadily
increased in popularity. It is nestled at the base of the foothills
which provides protection from the wind, besides a lovely
location. Since they have installed a new sprinkler system it is
one of the greenest courses around. The course is rated 68.7 for
the Men, and 71.1 for the Women. Men's yardage is 6281, par
71, and Women's yardage is 5428, par 71.

Valley Gardens Golf Course

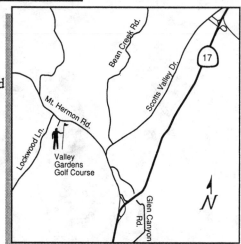

263 Mount Hermon Road
Scotts Valley, CA 95066

(408) 438-3058

9 Hole Course

Green Fees:

	Weekdays	Weekends
9 Holes:	$7.00	$9.00
18 Holes:	$15.00	$17.00

Twilight Rate: n.a.
Senior Discount: Limited to Wednesdays

Outfitting:

Golf Cars - 9 Holes: n.a.	Golf Cars - 18 Holes: n.a.
Pull Carts: $1.50	Clubs: $4.00

Lessons & More:

Club Pro: Jerry Imel   Lessons: 5 for $85
This course offers a Practice Putting Green, but no Chipping
Green or Driving Range. They have a new Pro Shop and Snack
Bar. Reservations for weekends can be made on the prior
Saturday or Sunday. Their least busy day of the week is Tues-
day.

Facts & Figures:

Valley Gardens Golf Course only measures 1765 yards from the
Men's Tees and 1557 yards from the Ladies' Tees. Four of the
holes have water hazards; on the 8th hole you must drive over
one to reach the green. This is a beautiful, well manicured, tree
lined course. They boast that their greens are among the best in
the county. Par for the course is 31. It is rated 56.5 from the
Men's Tees and 55 from the Ladies' Tees.

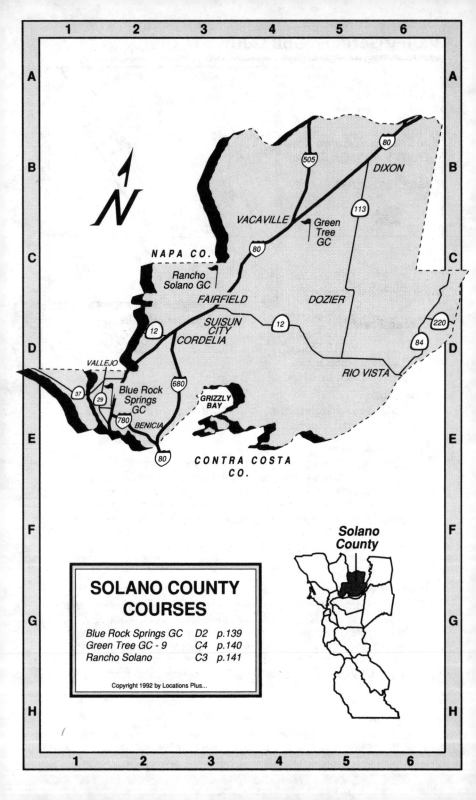

SOLANO COUNTY COURSES

Copyright 1992 by Locations Plus...

Blue Rock Springs Municipal Golf Course

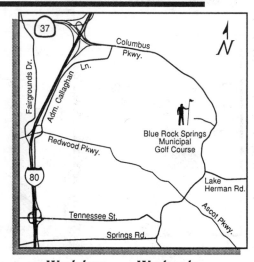

Columbus Parkway
Vallejo, CA 94590

(707) 643-8476

18 Hole Course

Green Fees

		Weekdays	Weekends
	9 Holes:	n.a.	n.a
	18 Holes:	$8.00	$11.00
Twilight Rate:		$4.00	$5.00
Senior Discount: n.a.			

Outfitting:

Golf Cars - 9 Holes: Golf Cars - 18 Holes: $14.00
Pull Carts: $2.00   Clubs: $5.00

Lessons & More:

Club Pro: Ralph W. Harris   Lessons: $20.00 / Lesson
Blue Rock Springs Municipal Golf Course offers a Practice Putting
Green and a Chipping Green, but no Driving Range. The
Rentrows Coffee Shop is open from 6 a.m. until 7 p.m. for your
convenience. Their Pro Shop carries a full line of golf merchandise. Weekend reservations can be made on the prior Tuesday,
for weekdays they can be made seven days in advance.

Facts & Figures:

In 1938 Blue Rock Springs Municipal opened as a 9 hole course
and was expanded to 18 holes in 1946. Once again, they are
working on adding another 18 holes as well as working on the
existing 18. The course is open for play. Yardage from the
Men's Tees is 6091, rated 69.4, par 72. From the Ladies' Tees it is
5894 yards long, rated 72.7, par 73. The course record of 63 is
held by Jeff Wilson.

Green Tree Golf Course

999 Leisure Town Rd.
Vacaville, CA 95688

(707) 448-1420

27 Hole Course

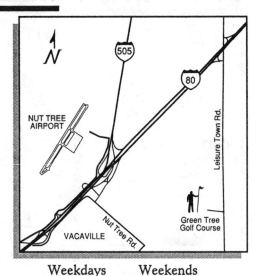

Green Fees

	Weekdays	Weekends
9 Holes:	*$5.00	*$6.00
18 Holes:	$11.00	$16.00
Twilight Rate:	$7.00	$9.00
Senior Discount: $1.00 off		

Outfitting:

Golf Cars - 9 Holes: *$10.00   Golf Cars - 18 Holes: $16.00
   Pull Carts: $2.00   Clubs: n.a.

Lessons & More:

Club Pro: Kelly Adams   **Lessons:** $20 / 45 Minutes
At Green Tree Golf Course you will find a Practice Putting Green,
Chipping Green and a Driving Range. Bucket prices: $1.50 -
$3.50. Their Snack Bar is open from 6 a.m. until 8 p.m. daily,
assorted beverages are sold. The Pro Shop carries a complete line
of golf accessories. Reservations can be made one week in
advance. *9 Hole rates apply to the 9 hole course only.

Facts & Figures:

Green Tree Golf Course is 25 years old and originally consisted of
only 3 holes. Now they have a 9 hole course which plays for
1053 yards and has a par of 29 and a championship 18 hole
course with three sets of tees. From the Blue Championship Tees
total yardage is 6370, from the White Tees it is 5906 and from the
Red Tees it is 5318. Course ratings are: 69.1, 67.1 and 68.2,
respectively. Overall par for the course is 71. Here at Green Tree
they have improved the overall condition of the course, their
greens are beautifully maintained. The mostly flat, wide fairways
offer good lies if you stay out of the trees.

140

Rancho Solano

3250 Rancho Solano
   Pkwy.
Fairfield, CA 94533

(707 429-4653

18 Hole Course

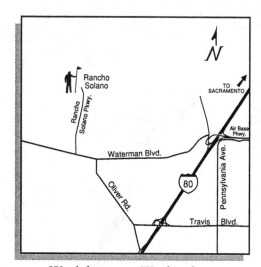

TO SACRAMENTO

Green Fees

	Weekdays	Weekends
9 Holes:	n.a.	n.a.
18 Holes:	$22.00	$27.00
Twilight Rate: 9 Holes	$8.50	$11.00
Senior Discount: n.a.		

Outfitting:

Golf Cars - 9 Holes: $11.00   Golf Cars - 18 Holes: $21.00
      Pull Carts: $3.00   Clubs: $10.00

Lessons & More:

Club Pro: Dale Bradley   Lessons: $25 / 30 Minutes
This 18 hole course has a Practice Putting Green, Chipping Green
and a Driving Range. Bucket prices range from $2.25 to $4.25.
There is a full restaurant, lounge and snack bar available. Their
Pro Shop's inventory is extensive. Reservations can be made 7
days in advance, beginning at 6:00 a.m. Their least busy time is
early on weekdays. There are 4 PGA professionals on the
teaching staff.

Facts & Figures:

This championship, 18 hole public course, designed by Gary
Roger Baird, Inc., opened on March 3, 1990. The layout of the
course is interesting as well as challenging as there is no lack of
sand or water. Their greens are tremendous in size, undulating
and quick. Residential property surround portions of the course.
Overall Par is 72. Yardages range from 5206 from the Ladies'
Tees to 6705 from the Championship Tees. The ratings and
slopes are: Blue 72.9/129, White 70.7/125, Gold 68.5/120 and
Red 69.6/117. There are 4 par 3 holes, 10 par 4 holes and 4 par 5
holes.

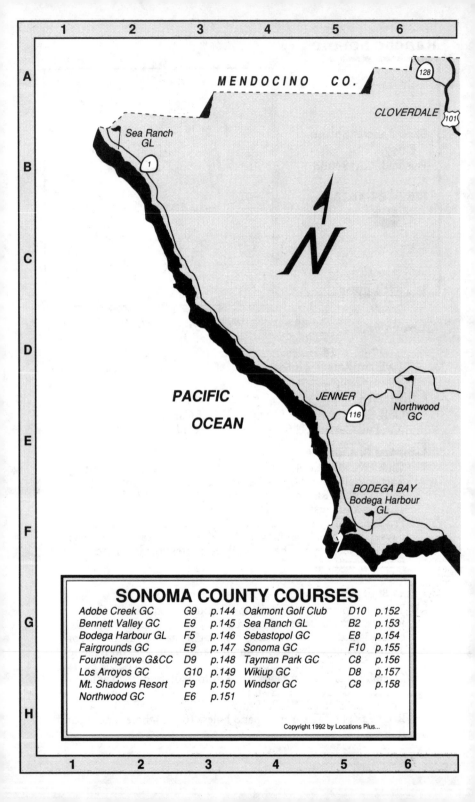

SONOMA COUNTY COURSES

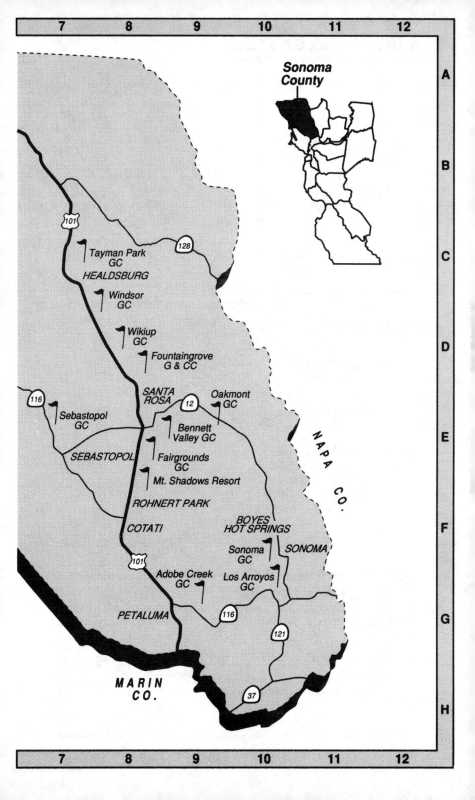

Adobe Creek Golf Club

1901 Frates Road
Petaluma, CA 94954

(707) 765-3000

18 Hole Course

Green Fees:

	Weekdays	Weekends
9 Holes:	n.a.	n.a.
18 Holes:	$45.00	$55.00
Twilight Rates:	$27.50	$32.50
Senior Discount: n.a.		

Outfitting:

Golf Cars - 9 Holes:	Golf Cars - 18 Holes: Included
Pull Carts: n.a.	Clubs: $20.00

Lessons & More:

Club Pro: Dana Banke   Lessons: $25 / 30 Minutes
Adobe Creek offers a Practice Putting Green, Chipping Green and
a Driving Range. Bucket price: $2.50 - $3.00. There is a full
restaurant and lounge available. Restaurant hours: 7:00 a.m. until
6:00 p.m. A Pro Shop provides a good selection of golf equipment. Reservations can be made 2 weeks in advance.
Mandatory Golf Car included in Green Fee.

Facts & Figures:

Robert Trent Jones, II designed this links style course which
opened on July 28, 1990. From the four tee choices available, the
yardages range from 6825 to 5027. The ratings and slopes are:
Gold 72.9/132, Blue 70.1/127, White 67.6/121 and Red 68.3/115.
Par for the Course is 72. You will play on well defined narrow
fairways, and smooth, fast greens. Water will come into play on
8 of the holes. This new championship course is worth a visit.

Bennett Valley Golf Course

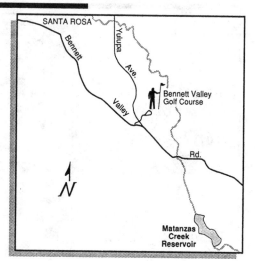

3330 Yulupa Avenue
Santa Rosa, CA 95405

(707) 528-3673

18 Hole Course

Green Fees:

	Weekdays	Weekends
9 Holes:	$6.00	$8.00
18 Holes:	$9.00	$12.00

Twilight Rates: After 2:00 p.m., same as 9 Hole Fee.
Senior Discount: $6.00 weekdays only, no holidays.

Outfitting:

Golf Cars - 9 Holes: Golf Cars - 18 Holes: $18.00
        Pull Carts: $2.00   Clubs: $8.00

Lessons & More:

Club Pro: Bob Borowicz   **Lessons:** $22 / 30 Minutes
Bennett Valley offers a Practice Putting Green and a Driving
Range. Bucket prices: $1.75 - $3.50.. Their cafe is open from
sunrise until 4 p.m. daily, a cocktail lounge is also available. The
Golf Shop carries a full line of merchandise. Weekend reservations can be made on the prior Saturday beginning at daybreak,
for weekdays one week in advance.

Sonoma County

Facts & Figures:

Any experienced level of golfer will find this eighteen hole
championship course in Santa Rosa challenging. It is rated 70.6
from the Championship Blue Tees, 69.0 from the White Tees,
and 72.5 from the Red Tees, Slope: 116. The course plays for a
total of 6583 yards. Men's par is 72, Ladies' par is 75. The
course record stands at 61. You will encounter water hazards on
holes #1, 7, 15, and 16. Bennett Valley Golf Course regularly
hosts the Santa Rosa City Championship, both Adult and Junior.

Bodega Harbour Golf Links

21301 Heron Drive
Bodega Bay, CA 94923

(707) 875-3538

18 Hole Course

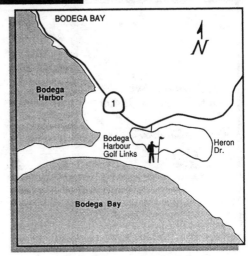

Green Fees:

	Weekdays	Weekends
9 Holes:	$20.00	$30.00
18 Holes:	$35.00	$53.00

Twilight Rates: $25.00 includes golf car
Senior Discount: n.a.

Outfitting:

Golf Cars - 9 Holes: $8.00   Golf Cars - 18 Holes: $12.00*
Pull Carts: $3.00   Clubs: $20.00

Lessons & More:

Club Pro: Dennis Kalkowski   Lessons: $35 / Lesson
A Practice Putting Green is available for warm-up at Bodega
Harbour Golf Links, but no Driving Range or Chipping Green.
They have a full restaurant and lounge open daily. The Pro Shop
carries a full line of golf equipment. Reservations can be made 60
days in advance. *Golf Car fee based on each player.

Facts & Figures:

This championship golf course, designed by Robert Trent Jones,
Jr., originally opened as a nine hole course in 1976. The second
nine was completed in September of 1987. Golf Digest nomi-
nated this course for "Best New Resort Course - 1988." Yardages
range from 6220 from the Championship Tees to 4746 yards
from the Red Tees. Ratings and slopes are: Championship 71.6/
130, Middle Tees 68.0/125 and Forward Tees 68.7/120. Each
year it plays host to the North Coast Amateur Tournament. You
will enjoy the unique style of this Scottish style links course. The
maintenance has been upgraded to ensure the course's high
ranking.

Fairgrounds Golf Course

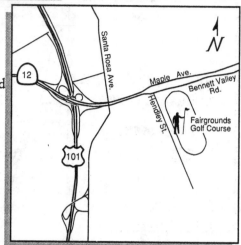

1350 Bennett Valley Road
Santa Rosa, CA 95404

(707) 546-2469

9 Hole Course

Green Fees:

	Weekdays	Weekends
9 Holes:	$6.00	$7.00
18 Holes:	$7.00	$8.00

Twilight Rates: After 5:00 $4.50
Senior Discount: $5.50 weekdays only.

Outfitting:

Golf Cars - 9 Holes: n.a.	Golf Cars - 18 Holes: n.a.
Pull Carts: $2.00	Clubs: $4.00

Lessons & More:

Club Pro: Wade Miller   **Lessons:** $30 / 60 Minutes
The Fairgrounds Golf Course offers a Practice Putting Green,
Chipping Green and a Driving Range. Large Bucket: $3.00, Small
Bucket: $2.00. Their Snack Bar is open from 7 a.m. until dark.
They have a new bar and remodeled Pro Shop. They have an
electric golf car available for seniors. Yearly Green Fee rates are
available. Reservations are not taken, first come, first served.

Facts & Figures:

Fairgrounds Golf Course opened in 1956. This is a public nine
hole golf course. It measures 1657 yards with a par of 29. There
are two par 4 holes and the rest are par 3's. This is a flat course
with two water hazards. What makes this course difficult are the
target greens. They have recently added a sandtrap and planted
more trees.

Sonoma
County

147

Fountaingrove Resort & Country Club

1525 Fountaingrove Pkwy.
Santa Rosa, CA 95403

(707) 579-4653

18 Hole Course

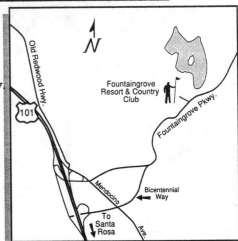

Green Fees:

	Weekdays	Weekends
9 Holes:	n.a.	n.a.
18 Holes:	$45.00	$65.00

Twilight Rates: n.a.
Senior Discount: n.a.

Outfitting:

Golf Cars - 9 Holes: Golf Cars - 18 Holes: Included
Pull Carts: n.a.   Clubs: $15.00

Lessons & More:

Club Pro: J. Michael Jonas   Lessons: $30 / 30 Minutes
There is a Practice Putting Green and a Driving Range sporting new mats for all weather use. The Sonoma Grill, a full service restaurant and lounge, and a new indoor Snack Bar are available. The Pro Shop is fully stocked. Reservations can be made seven days in advance beginning at 7:30 a.m. Mandatory Golf Cars included in Green Fees

Facts & Figures:

This course, designed by Ted Robinson, opened in 1985. This is a semi-private,18 hole championship course located on the historic Fountaingrove Ranch. This is a very hilly course, beautifully landscaped with plenty of trees. It also has a fairly large lake sitting right in the center which will provide a hazard on 4 of the holes. From the Blue Tees it is 6797 yards long, rated 72.8, slope 132. They say you will use every club in your bag by the time you complete a round of golf at Fountaingrove.

Los Arroyos Golf Course

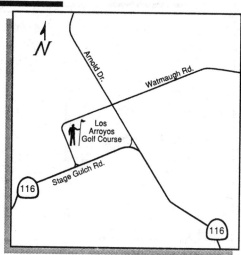

5000 Stage Gulch Road
Sonoma, CA 95476

(707) 938-8835

9 Hole Course

Green Fees:

	Weekdays	Weekends
9 Holes:	$7.00	$9.00
18 Holes:	$9.00	$10.00
Twilight Rates:	$3.00	$7.00
Senior Discount: $5.00 on Wednesdays		

Outfitting:

Golf Cars - 9 Holes: n.a.   Golf Cars - 18 Holes: n.a.
Pull Carts: $2.00   Clubs: $5.00

Lessons & More:

Club Pro: Wade Miller   **Lessons:** $30 / 60 Minutes
Los Arroyos Golf Course offers a Driving Range which they have just expanded, as their warm-up facility. Bucket price: $3.00 They have a light Snack Bar and Pro Shop carrying a nice assortment of golf equipment. They do not take reservations, first come, first served.

Facts & Figures:

This 9 hole course which opened in 1971 has recently changed hands. They have installed a new irrigation system and another lake last year to enhance the course. It will play for a total of 1600 yards and has a par of 29. There are two par 4's and the rest are par 3's. The course is located out in the open and runs pretty flat. There is a lovely creek running toward the back of the course and a nice size lake sitting right in the middle. The fairways are 25 yards wide, the greens are small and rolling. Most golfers will find this little course a challenge.

Mountain Shadows Resort

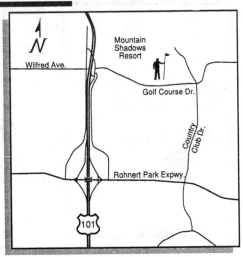

100 Golf Course Drive
Rohnert Park, CA 94928

(707) 584-7766

<u>36 Hole Course</u>

Green Fees:

	Weekdays	Weekends
9 Holes:	n.a.	n.a.
18 Holes:	$18/*$29	$30/*$45

Twilight Rates: $13 So./$15 No. - Winter 1 p.m. / Summer 4 p.m.
Senior Discount: $13.00 on South Course, $15.00 on North

Outfitting:

Golf Cars - 9 Holes: Golf Cars - 18 Holes: $22.00
Pull Carts: $3.00   Clubs: $10.00

Lessons & More:

Club Pro: Greg Anderson   Lessons: $25 / Lesson
A Practice Putting Green and a Driving Range are available at
Mountain Shadows. Large Bucket: $3.50. Their restaurant is
open from 6 a.m. until 9 p.m., a cocktail lounge is also available.
The Pro Shop carries a full line of golf equipment. Reservations
can be made one week in advance. Their busiest day of the week
is Friday, least busy day is Monday.
*On the North Course Golf Car included in Green Fee.

Facts & Figures:

Mountain Shadows Resort provides 2, 18 hole golf courses. The
North Course is their championship course, offering 4 sets of tee
boxes. The yardages range from 7035 from the Gold, rated 72.1,
down to 5503 from the Red, rated 70.4 The South Course, with
its very narrow fairways is 6500 yards long, rated 69.7, par is 72.
Both of these courses are well maintained allowing the golfer an
enjoyable outing.

Northwood Golf Course

19400 Highway 116
Monte Rio, CA 95462

(707) 865-1116

9 Hole Course

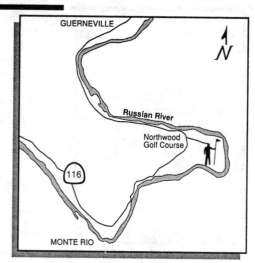

Green Fees:

	Weekdays	Weekends
9 Holes:	$12.00	$15.00
18 Holes:	$18.00	$23.00

Twilight Rates: $6.00
Senior Discount: 10 rounds for $80.00 Monday thru Friday

Outfitting:

Golf Cars - 9 Holes: $10.00   Golf Cars - 18 Holes: $16.00
Pull Carts: $2.00   Clubs: $5.00

Lessons & More:

Club Pro: John Moore   **Lessons:** $25 / 45 Minutes
Northwood Golf Course offers a Practice Putting Green, Chipping Green and a Driving Range as their warm-up facilities. The Northwood Restaurant and Lounge is open from 10 a.m. until 10 p.m. The Pro Shop will be able to fill your golfing needs. Reservations can be made two weeks in advance. Their busiest day of the week is Saturday, least busy day is Tuesday.

Facts & Figures:

Northwood Golf Course was designed by the famed golf course architect, Alister Mackenzie in 1928. During the 1950's this course played host to such notables as Bing Crosby, Phil Harris and Lowell Thomas. This nine hole course runs for a total of 2875 yards and has a par of 36. Huge redwoods and fir trees provide the backdrop for this lovely course located in the wine country.

Sonoma
County

151

Oakmont Golf Club

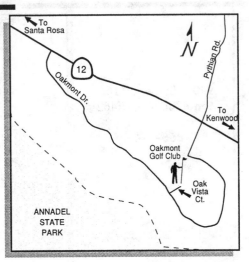

7025 Oakmont Drive
Santa Rosa, CA 95405
(707) 538-2454-East
(707) 539-0414-West

<u>18 Hole Courses</u>

Green Fees:

	Weekdays	Weekends
9 Holes:	$12/*$15	$15/*$20
18 Holes:	$17/*$22	$22/*$30

Twilight Rates: 9 Hole Fee at 2:00 p.m.
Senior Discount: n.a.   * West Course Fees

Outfitting:

Golf Cars - 9 Holes:	Golf Cars - 18 Holes: $22.00
Pull Carts: $3.00	Clubs: $5.00

Lessons & More:

Club Pro: Dean James   **Lessons:** $25 / 30 Minutes
At Oakmont Golf Club - West you will find a Practice Putting
Green and a Driving Range. Bucket price: $2.50 - $3.00. The
Chalet at Oakmont is open daily for lunch and dinner. The Pro
shop carries a complete line of golf equipment. Reservations can
be made one week in advance. At Oakmont - East there is a very
limited Pro Shop. Vending machines provide the refreshments.

Facts & Figures:

  This course is located in what is regionally known as the "Valley
of the Moon." Homes have been built in recent years surrounding most of the course. The West Course is their championship
course that measures 6379 yards long, rated 70.4, slope 115.
From the White it is 6059 yards, 69.0/112, and from the Red it is
5573, 71.9/128. The Woodstock Open is held here each year.
The East Course is 4293 yards long from the White Tees, rated
59.8, from the Red Tees it is 4067, rated 63.4, slope 95.

Sea Ranch Golf Links

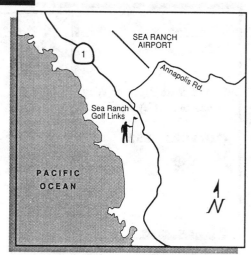

49300 Hwy. 1
Sea Ranch, CA 95497

(707) 785-2467

9 Hole Course

Green Fees:

	Weekdays	Weekends
9 Holes:	$17.00	$22.00
18 Holes:	$22.00	$33.00

Twilight Rates: n.a.
Senior Discount: n.a.

Outfitting:

Golf Cars - 9 Holes: $15.00   Golf Cars - 18 Holes: $24.00
     Pull Carts: $2.00   Clubs: $15.00 / $25.00

Lessons & More:

Club Pro: Rich Bland   **Lessons:** $30 / 30 Minutes
The Sea Ranch Golf Links offers a Practice Putting Green and a
Driving Range. Large Bucket: $6.00, Small Bucket: $3.00. The
Sea Ranch Lodge Restaurant is open daily for your convenience
along with a Snack Bar. The Pro Shop offers a nice selection of
golf equipment. Reservations can be made 30 days in advance.

Facts & Figures:

This 9 hole course, designed by Robert Muir Graves, was
constructed in 1973. The course measures 6740 yards long and
has a par of 73 when playing 18 holes. It also provides three sets
of tees. The course is rated 73.5 and has a slope of 133, the 13th
highest in Northern California. The course record is held by Rich
Bland with a 69. In 1991 Golf Digest rated Sea Ranch Golf Links
as one of the Top 5, 9 hole golf courses in Northern California.

Sebastopol Golf Course

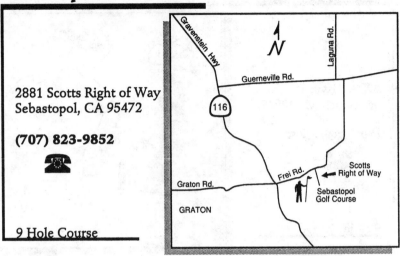

2881 Scotts Right of Way
Sebastopol, CA 95472

(707) 823-9852

9 Hole Course

Green Fees:

	Weekdays	Weekends
9 Holes:	$7.00	$9.00
18 Holes:	$8.00	$10.00

Twilight Rates: n.a.
Senior Discount: $6.00 Wednesday only

Outfitting:

Golf Cars - 9 Holes: $7.00   Golf Cars - 18 Holes: $10.00
        Pull Carts: $2.00   Clubs: $3.00

Lessons & More:

Club Pro: Lee Farris   Lessons: n.a.
Sebastopol Golf Course has a Practice Putting Green, but no Chipping Green or Driving Range. The Snack Bar is open from dawn to dusk for your convenience. The Pro Shop carries sufficient equipment to help fill your golfing needs. Reservations are not taken, first come, first served.

Facts & Figures:

This nine hole course was constructed by Sam Farris and Son in 1958. It has been a family run facility ever since. It is located just 3 miles north of Sebastopol. This well maintained course plays for 1663 yards. Par is 31 / 33. Four of the holes have a par 4 if you play from the Men's Tees and from the Ladies' Tees, six of the holes are par 4's. There is a water hazard around the green on the 8th hole. Sebastopol annually hosts the Apple Blossom Tournament during the first week in April.

154

Sonoma Golf Club

17700 Arnold Drive
Sonoma, CA 95426

(707) 996-0300

18 Hole Course

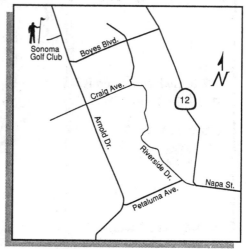

Green Fees:

	Weekdays	Weekends
9 Holes:	n.a.	n.a.
18 Holes:	$60.00	$80.00
Twilight Rates:	$30.00	$40.00
Senior Discount: n.a.		

Outfitting:

Golf Cars - 9 Holes: Included   Golf Cars - 18 Holes: Included
Pull Carts: Clubs: $30.00

Lessons & More:

Club Pro: Ron Blum   **Lessons:** $30 / 30 Minutes
There is a Practice Putting Green, Chipping Green and Driving
Range available. Bucket prices: $3.00 - $5.00. Their full restaurant is open from dawn to dusk. The Pro Shop carries a full line
of merchandise. Reservations can be made up to two weeks in
advance beginning at day break. Golf Car included in Green Fee.

Facts & Figures:

Sonoma Golf Club, built in 1926, was designed by Sam Whiting
and known as Sonoma National. In 1988-89 it underwent a 10
million dollar renovation with Robert Muir Graves helping to
keep the original design. All greens have been built to USGA
specs, trees were planted, fairways rebuilt, 2 new lakes were
added and an irrigation system installed. The course offers 4 sets
of tees. Yardages, ratings and slopes are: Blue: 7069, 74.9/135,
White 6783, 72.2/130, Gold: 6051, 69.9/126 and Red: 5519, 71.5/
128. Overall course par is 72. The greens are hand mowed daily
and the fairways are mowed six days a week.

Tayman Park Golf Course

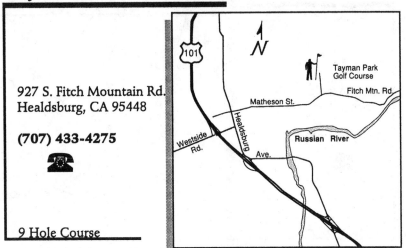

927 S. Fitch Mountain Rd.
Healdsburg, CA 95448

(707) 433-4275

9 Hole Course

Green Fees:

	Weekdays	Weekends
9 Holes:	$9.00	$11.00
18 Holes:	$11.00	$13.00

Twilight Rates: n.a.
Senior Discount: $7.00 Weekdays only

Outfitting:

Golf Cars - 9 Holes: $9.00   Golf Cars - 18 Holes: $16.00
Pull Carts: $2.00   Clubs: $5.00

Lessons & More:

Club Pro: Mike Ash   Lessons: $20 / Lesson
A Practice Putting Green is available at Tayman Park, but no
Chipping Green or Driving Range. The Tayman Park Bar and
Grill is open from 6 a.m. until 8 p.m. for your convenience. The
Pro Shop handles golfing accessories to help in filling your
immediate needs. Reservations can be made two weeks in
advance.

Facts & Figures:

This public nine hole course gives you a choice of tees on some
of the holes when playing a full eighteen. The length of the
course is 5349 yards long from the Men's Tees and is rated 64.8.
From the Women's Tees it is 4952 yards long and is rated 68.4
Overall par is 70. Only one of the holes is a par 5; there are two
par 3's and the rest are par 4's. Except for one fairly severe
dogleg, most of the holes are a straight shot to the green. You
have to shoot directly over water on two of the holes.

Wikiup Golf Course

5001 Carriage Lane
Santa Rosa, CA 95403

(707) 546-8787

9 Hole Course

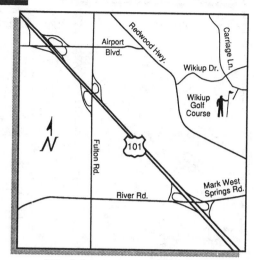

Green Fees:

	Weekdays	Weekends
9 Holes:	$7.00	$9.00
18 Holes:	$10.00	$12.00

Twilight Rates: n.a.
Senior Discount: $7.00 for 18 holes - Weekdays

Outfitting:

Golf Cars - 9 Holes: $9.00   Golf Cars - 18 Holes: $12.00
    Pull Carts: $2.00   Clubs: $3.00

Lessons & More:

Club Pro: n.a.   Lessons: n.a.
A Practice Putting Green is available at Wikiup Golf Course, but
no Chipping Green or Driving Range. The Snack Shop is open
from 7 a.m. until 6 p.m. serving tasty sandwiches and assorted
beverages, including beer and wine. The Pro Shop carries a
limited assortment of golf accessories. Reservations are not
taken, first come, first served.

Facts & Figures:

This 9 hole public course opened in 1963. There is a little lake
sitting across the fairway on the 2nd hole which also presents a
lateral water hazard on holes #5, 6, 7, and 8. It is a pleasant
course to play, well maintained, with fairly nice size greens.
Total yardage, if playing eighteen holes, is 3254. It is rated 54.0.
Men's par is 58, Women's par is 60. All the holes are par 3's
except for #2, and #8. The 8th is a par 5 for the Ladies.

Sonoma County

157

Windsor Golf Club

6555 Skylane Boulevard
Windsor, CA 95492

(707) 838-7888

18 Hole Course

Green Fees:

	Weekdays	Weekends
9 Holes:	n.a.	n.a.
18 Holes:	$19.00	$29.00
Twilight Rates:	$13.00	$19.00

Senior Discount: $11.00 Mon., Tues. and Wed.

Outfitting:

Golf Cars - 9 Holes:	Golf Cars - 18 Holes: $20.00
Pull Carts: $2.00	Clubs: $10.00

Lessons & More:

Club Pro: Charlie Gibson   **Lessons:** $20 / 30 Minutes
Windsor Golf Club offers a Practice Putting Green and a Driving
Range. Bucket prices range from $1 to $3. Their Snack Bar is
open from 7 a.m. until 7 p.m., daily. Their Pro Shop will be able
to fill most of your golfing needs. Reservations can be made
seven days in advance. Their least busy day is Tuesday.

Facts & Figures:

This 18 hole championship course sits on 120 acres of rolling
countryside. There is plenty of room between fairways, enough
for 5 lakes, a small stream and a couple of marshes. The greens
are small and with all of natures enhancements, this course offers
a challenge. It measures 6650 yards long from the Championship
Tees and has a rating of 72.3. From the Blue Tees: 6169 yds.
rated 70.1/121, Regular Tees: 5628 yds. rated 67.0/118, Forward
Tees: 5116 yds. rated 69.3/125. Par for the course is 72. This
course hosts the Ben Hogan Tournament, the Santa Rosa Open
and the Hot Air Balloon Classic.

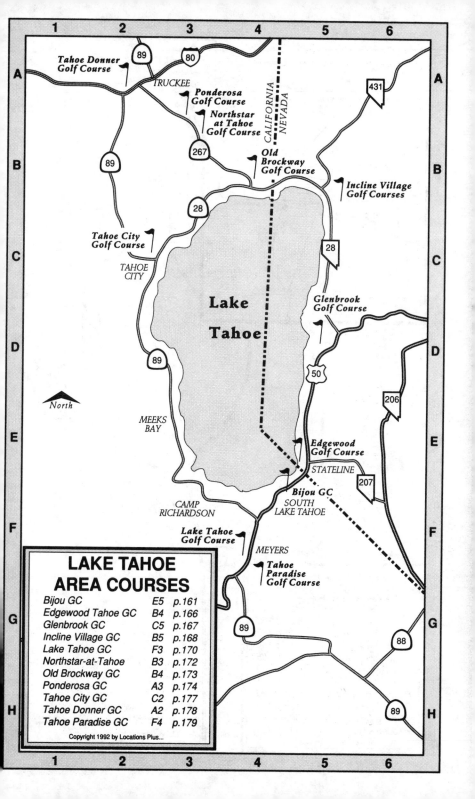

LAKE TAHOE AREA COURSES

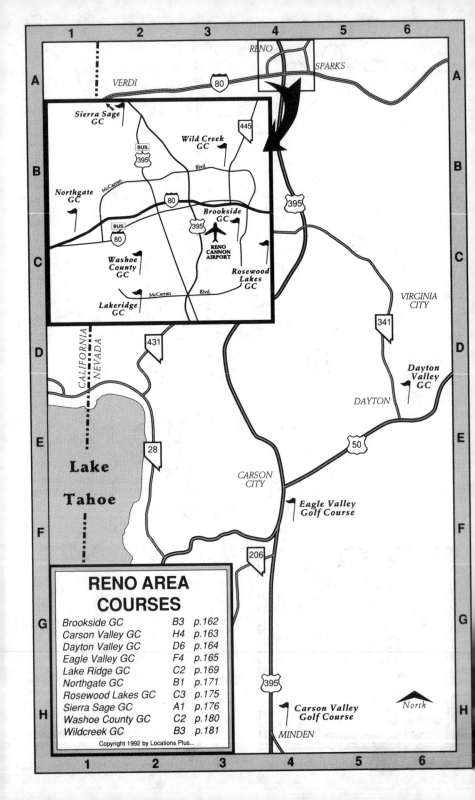

RENO

SPARKS

VERDI

1 2 3 4 5 6

A

Sierra Sage
GC

445

Wild Creek
GC

BUS.
395

Blvd.

Northgate
GC

McCarran

80

Brookside
GC

395

RENO
CANNON
AIRPORT

Washoe
County
GC

Rosewood
Lakes
GC

McCarran

Blvd.

Lakeridge
GC

B

395

VIRGINIA
CITY

341

431

Dayton
Valley
GC

C

CALIFORNIA
NEVADA

DAYTON

D

28

50

Lake

Tahoe

CARSON
CITY

Eagle Valley
Golf Course

E

F

206

RENO AREA
COURSES

Brookside GC	B3	p.162
Carson Valley GC	H4	p.163
Dayton Valley GC	D6	p.164
Eagle Valley GC	F4	p.165
Lake Ridge GC	C2	p.169
Northgate GC	B1	p.171
Rosewood Lakes GC	C3	p.175
Sierra Sage GC	A1	p.176
Washoe County GC	C2	p.180
Wildcreek GC	B3	p.181

Copyright 1992 by Locations Plus...

395

North

Carson Valley
Golf Course

MINDEN

G

H

1 2 3 4 5 6

Bijou Golf Course

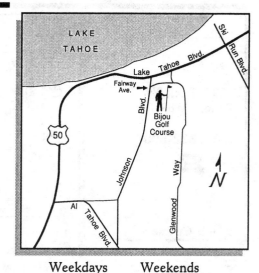

3464 Fairway Ave.
So. Lake Tahoe, CA
96150
(916) 544-5500

9 Hole Course

Green Fees:

		Weekdays	Weekends
9 Holes:		$8.00	$8.00
18 Holes:		$14.00	$14.00

Twilight Rate: Yes
Senior Discount: n.a.

Outfitting:

Golf Cars - 9 Holes: n.a.	Golf Cars - 18 Holes: n.a.
Pull Carts: $2.00	Clubs: $2.00

Lessons & More:

Club Pro: n.a.   Lessons: n.a.

Bijou Golf Course provides a Driving Range Net which is free with Green Fees, otherwise there is a $1.00 charge. A Snack Bar is open for your convenience. The course is closed from October 15th to April 15th.

Facts & Figures:

This 9 hole public course is situated in an open meadow. It is a pleasant course to play, easy to walk and offers some scenic views. The course plays for a total of 2030 yards and has a par of 32. There are 5 par 4 holes and 4 par 3s. They have recently installed a new irrigation system and have made other improvements to this popular course.

Tahoe-Reno Area

161

Brookside Municipal Golf Course

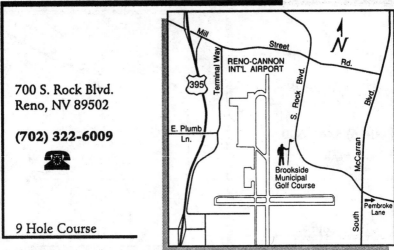

700 S. Rock Blvd.
Reno, NV 89502

(702) 322-6009

9 Hole Course

Green Fees:

	Weekdays	Weekends
9 Holes:	$5.00	$5.00
18 Holes:	$10.00	$10.00

Twilight Rate: n.a.
Senior Discount: $6.00 for 18 Holes

Outfitting:

Golf Cars - 9 Holes: $8.00	Golf Cars - 18 Holes: $18.00
Pull Carts: $1.00	Clubs: $5.00

Lessons & More:

Club Pro: n.a.   Lessons: n.a.

Brookside offers a Practice Putting Green and a netted driving area as their warm-up facilities. They have a Snack Bar open for your convenience. Their Pro Shop's inventory is very limited. This course is open all year.

Facts & Figures:

This 9 hole municipal course is located right next to the Reno-Cannon International Airport. It is a regulation 9 hole course which measures 2882 yards, has a par of 35 and slope rating of 107. This is a easy to walk, easy to play course that is favored by the seniors. The greens are in excellent shape.

Carson Valley Golf Course

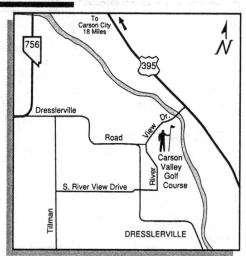

1027 Riverview Dr.
Gardnerville, NV 89410

(702) 265-3181

18 Hole Course

Green Fees:

	Weekdays	Weekends
9 Holes:	$10.00	$10.00
18 Holes:	$16.00	$16.00

Twilight Rate: n.a.
Senior Discount: n.a.

Outfitting:

Golf Cars - 9 Holes: $10.00   Golf Cars - 18 Holes: $16.00
Pull Carts: $1.50 per 9   Clubs: $7.50 / $10.00

Lessons & More:

Club Pro: Janelle Brown   Lessons: $25 / 60 Minutes
A Practice Putting Green, Chipping Green and Driving Range are
available. Bucket prices: $3.00 - $3.50. Their restaurant serves
everything, but breakfast. The Pro Shop carries a limited supply
of golf equipment. Reservations can be made one week in
advance.

Facts & Figures:

Carson Valley Golf Course is private, but open to the public.
This 18 hole course measures 5759 yards from the Blue Tees and
5283 from the Red. Par is 71/72. The challenges here are the
small greens and narrow fairways occasionally obstructed by
trees. You will find water coming into play on all, but two, of the
holes. It is easy walking due to the lack of hills. They have been
busy rebuilding their tee boxes.

Tahoe-Reno Area

163

Dayton Valley Country Club

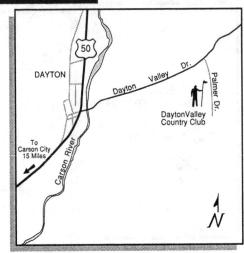

51 Palmer Drive
Dayton, NV 89403

(702) 246-7888

18 Hole Course

Green Fees:

	Weekdays	Weekends
9 Holes:	n.a.	n.a.
18 Holes:	$50.00	$50.00

Twilight Rate: n.a.
Senior Discount: n.a.

Outfitting:

Golf Cars - 9 Holes:	Golf Cars - 18 Holes: Included
Pull Carts: n.a.	Clubs: $20.00

Lessons & More:

Club Pro: Jim Kepler   Lessons: $40 / Lesson
Dayton Valley offers a Practice Putting Green, Chipping Green and a Driving Range. Bucket price: $3.00 They have a Snack Bar open daily. Dinner is served on Friday and Saturday. The Pro Shop carries a nice assortment of golf equipment. Reservations can be made 8 days in advance. Golf Cars are mandatory, they are included in the Green Fees.

Facts & Figures:

This new championship course open in May of 1991. It has already received good reviews by the professionals. The course consists of contoured fairways with specified landing areas, the greens are medium sized. From the Championship Tees it will play for a whopping 7161 yards. This course has already played host to the Nevada State Amateur and for the first time in Nevada, the United States Amateur Qualifier.

Eagle Valley Golf Course

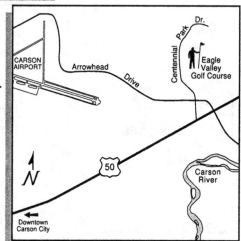

3999 Centennial Park Dr.
Carson City, NV 89706

(702) 887-2380

36 Hole Course

Green Fees:

	Weekdays	Weekends
9 Holes:	$8.00	$8.00
18 Holes:	$14 / $30*	$14 / $30*

Twilight Rate: $7 on East Course and $15 on West Course
Senior Discount: n.a.

Outfitting:

Golf Cars - 9 Holes: $9.00   Golf Cars - 18 Holes: $17.00
Pull Carts: Clubs:

Lessons & More:

Club Pro: Gary Bushman   Lessons: $30 / Lesson
Eagle Valley offers a Practice Putting Green, Chipping Green and a Driving Range. Bucket prices: $3.00 - $5.00 They have a full restaurant open from 6 a.m. until 6 p.m., April through Sept. The Pro Shop is complete. From October 1st to March 1st Green Fees are $25.00. Reservations are taken on Friday's after 3 p.m. for following Monday through Sunday. *Golf Cars are mandatory on the West Course, they are included in the Green Fees.

Facts & Figures:

The "East" Course is the older of the two courses and is also the easiest to play. The fairways are wide and very forgiving, great for the beginner. It measures 6658 yards long, ratings and slopes are: Blue - 68.7/117, White - 67.3/114, Red - 72.3/123. The "West" Course is only 5 years old and was designed to give the best golfers a challenge as most links style courses do. The West course is just a little longer, ratings and slopes are: Blue 71.5/127, White 69.0/123 and Red 68.5/116. They are able to keep their course green by using reclaimed water.

165

Edgewood Tahoe Golf Course

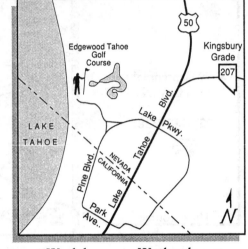

Hwy. 50 & Lake Pkwy.
Lake Tahoe, NV 89449

(702) 588-3566

18 Hole Course

Green Fees:

	Weekdays	Weekends
9 Holes:	n.a.	n.a.
18 Holes:	$100.00	$100.00

Twilight Rate: n.a.
Senior Discount: n.a.

Outfitting:

Golf Cars - 9 Holes:	Golf Cars - 18 Holes: Included
Pull Carts: n.a.	Clubs: $20.00

Lessons & More:

Club Pro: Lou Eiguren **Lessons:** $30 / $50

This course provides a Practice Putting Green, Chipping Green and a Driving Range. Bucket price: $3.00. Their facilities include a restaurant, lounge and Snack Bar, with hours from 7 a.m. until 10 p.m. The Pro Shop is complete. Reservations can be made up to two weeks in advance. Golf Cars are mandatory seven days a week.

Facts & Figures:

One look at this beautiful championship course and you will easily understand why it was ranked as one of the top 100 by Golf Digest. The rolling fairways and large greens are set among the tall pines. Lakes and streams abound. This 250 acre course provides 4 sets of tees to choose. Total yards from the Gold Championship Tees is 7491, rated 75.8, from the Blue Tees 6960 yards, rated 72.8, from the White 6544 yards, rated 70.9 and from the Red 5759 yards, rated 72.5. Overall par for the course is 72, course record is 64.

Glenbrook Golf Course

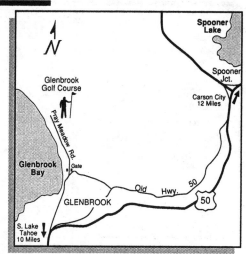

Pray Meadow Road
Glenbrook, NV 89413

(702) 749-5201

9 Hole Course

Green Fees:

	Weekdays	Weekends
9 Holes:		
18 Holes:	$37.00	$37.00
Twilight Rate: After 3:00	$25.00	$25.00
Senior Discount: n.a.		

Outfitting:

Golf Cars - 9 Holes: $10.00	Golf Cars - 18 Holes: $20.00
Pull Carts:	Clubs: $15.00

Lessons & More:

Club Pro: Warren MacCarty **Lessons:**
Glenbrook Golf Course provides a Practice Putting Green, and a Driving Range. They have a Snack Bar and lounge for your convenience. Their Pro Shop can help fill your golfing needs. This course is open mid-April to mid-October. Please check with the Pro Shop regarding golf lessons.

Facts & Figures:

Glenbrook is a public course within a private development. It was established in 1926 and is considered to be one of the finest 9 hole courses in the Tahoe area. Yardage based on 18 holes of play is 5318 from the Men's Tees, is rated 64. From the Ladies' Tees it is 4872, rated 65.8. Course par is 71/72. Ben Hogan played here in 1950 and shot 62 which still stands as the course record. Glenbrook offers some very scenic holes such as the 3rd green which is framed by Lake Tahoe. To reach the course take U.S. 50 to the Glenbrook turnoff, check in with the gatekeeper and follow Pray Meadow Road.

Tahoe-Reno Area

167

Incline Village Golf Resort

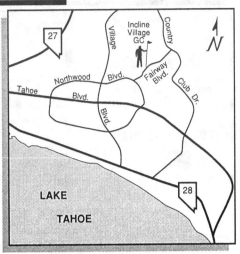

955 Fairway Blvd.
Incline Village, NV 89450
Championship Course
(702) 832-1144(5)

Executive Course
(702) 832-1150

36 Hole Course

Green Fees:

	Weekdays	Weekends
9 Holes:	n.a.	n.a.
18 Holes:	*$50 / $90	*$50 / $90

Twilight Rate: Yes
Senior Discount: n.a.

Outfitting:

Golf Cars - 9 Holes: Included   Golf Cars - 18 Holes: Included
Pull Carts: n.a.   Clubs: $25.00

Lessons & More:

Club Pro: **Randy Cooper   Lessons: $45 / Lesson
Both courses have Practice Putting Greens and there is a Driving
Range at the Championship Course. Bucket price: $3.50. Both
courses have Snack Bars serving a variety of food and beverages.
The Pro Shops have a nice assortment of golf equipment. These
courses are open May through October. The Dir. of Golf at the
Championship Course is John Hughes. **Club Pro at the Execu-
tive Course. *$50.00 are the Green Fees at the Executive
Course.

Facts & Figures:

Incline Village Resort consists of 2, 18 hole golf courses. The
Championship Course opened in 1964 and was designed by
Robert Trent Jones. It is 6910 yards long, rated 72.6, slope of 129
and has a par of 72. The Executive Course opened in 1969 and
was designed by Robert Trent Jones, Jr. This course is 3513 yards
long, rated 56.6, slope 94 and has a par of 58. You will need to
set aside 3 1/2 to 4 hours to play this incredibly challenging
executive course.

168

Copyright 1992 by Locations Plus...

Lake Ridge Golf Course

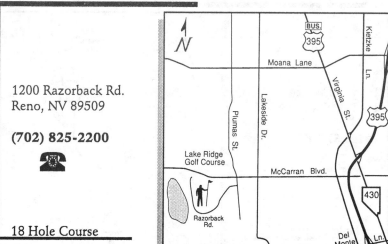

1200 Razorback Rd.
Reno, NV 89509

(702) 825-2200

18 Hole Course

Green Fees:

	Weekdays	Weekends
9 Holes:	n.a.	n.a.
18 Holes:	$46.00	$46.00

Twilight Rate: $28.00
Senior Discount: n.a.

Outfitting:

Golf Cars - 9 Holes: $10.00   Golf Cars - 18 Holes: $20.00
Pull Carts: n.a.   Clubs: $20.00

Lessons & More:

Club Pro: Paul Lane   Lessons: $30 / Lesson
This course provides Practice Putting Greens, a Chipping Green and a Driving Range. Bucket prices: $2.50 - $3.50. They have a Snack Bar open daily plus The 19th Hole Restaurant which is open every night except Sunday & Monday. The Pro Shop carries a nice assortment of golf equipment. Golf Cars are mandatory in-season only. Green Fees during off season are $28.00. Green Fees include Golf Cars.

Facts & Figures:

This championship, 18 hole, par 71 golf course was designed by Robert Trent Jones Jr. Their par 3, 15th hole features tees 120 feet above an island green which is set in Lake Stanley. The view of Reno and the surrounding mountains is enjoyed by the golfers as well as the home owners in the development that encircles the golf course. The entire course plays for a total of 6703 yards from the Blue Tees, 6140 from the White and 5159 from the Red. It is a challenging course for any experienced level of golfer.

Tahoe-Reno Area

169

Lake Tahoe Golf Course

Hwy. 50 West
So. Lake Tahoe, NV 95731

(916) 577-0788

18 Hole Course

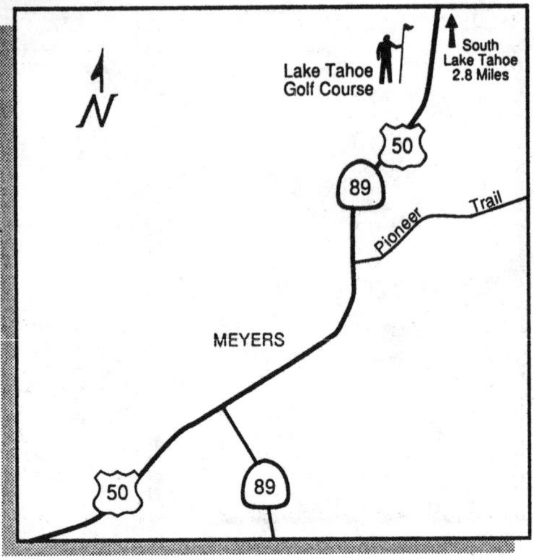

Green Fees:

	Weekdays	Weekends
9 Holes:	n.a.	n.a.
18 Holes:	$28.00	$39.00*

Twilight Rate: $21.00
Senior Discount: n.a.

Outfitting:

Golf Cars - 9 Holes: $12.00   Golf Cars - 18 Holes: $22.00
Pull Carts: $5.00   Clubs: $20.00

Lessons & More:

Club Pro: Dave Rowe   Lessons: $25 / Lesson
This course provides a Practice Putting Green, Chipping Green and a Driving Range. Bucket prices: $2.50 - $4.00. They have a Coffee Shop serving breakfast and lunch from 6 a.m. until 3 p.m. and a new Clubhouse. The Pro Shop carries an extensive inventory. Reservations can be made 30 days in advance with a credit card. Their busiest day is Saturday, least busy on Sunday p.m.
*Golf Car included in weekend fees.

Facts & Figures:

Lake Tahoe Golf Course is approximately 25 years old. It is a championship course that is well maintained. Its location provides the golfers with the beautiful views for which this area is so well known. The course is flat to gently rolling. It is considered a placement course, allowing little to no room for error on your golf shots. The course measures 6707 yards from the Blue Tees, 6169 from the White and 5687 from the Red. The course ratings and slopes are: 70.6/117, 67.9/110 and 70.1/115, respectively. Par is 71/72.

170

Northgate Golf Club

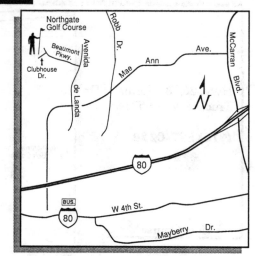

1111 Clubhouse Dr.
Reno, NV 89523

(702) 747-7577

18 Hole Course

Green Fees:

	Weekdays	Weekends
9 Holes:	n.a.	n.a.
18 Holes:	$37.00	$37.00

Twilight Rate: 9 Holes, $20.00 with cart
Senior Discount: n.a.

Outfitting:

Golf Cars - 9 Holes:	Included	Golf Cars - 18 Holes:	Included
Pull Carts:	n.a.	Clubs:	$20.00

Lessons & More:

Club Pro: Don Boyle   Lessons: $35 / 60 Minutes
Northgate Golf Club provides a Practice Putting Green, Chipping Green and a Driving Range. Bucket Price: $2.50. They provide a Snack Bar as well as a Pro Shop with a nice assortment of golf equipment. Reservations can be made seven days in advance. Golf Cars are mandatory on Sundays. This club offers Winter Rates. It is closed from the 15th of December to the 1st of February.

Facts & Figures:

This 18 hole championship course, which opened in 1988, used to be a stop for the Ben Hogan Tour. It is a links style course that sets it apart from others in the area. From the Blue Tees the course measures 6500 yards, rated 69.8 with a slope of 126. From the White Tees it is 6000 yards long, rated 67.5 with a slope of 122 and from the Red it is 5600 yards long, rated 70.3 with a slope of 127.

Northstar-at-Tahoe Resort Golf Course

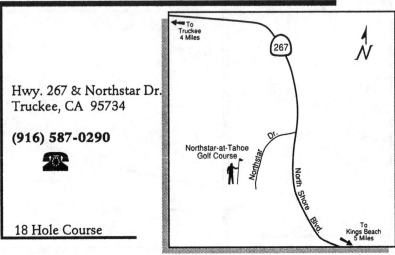

Hwy. 267 & Northstar Dr.
Truckee, CA 95734

(916) 587-0290

18 Hole Course

Green Fees:

		Weekdays	Weekends
9 Holes:			
18 Holes:		$49.00	$49.00

Twilight Rate: Yes
Senior Discount: Yes

Outfitting:

Golf Cars - 9 Holes: Golf Cars - 18 Holes: $11.00*
Pull Carts: n.a.   Clubs: $20.00

Lessons & More:

Club Pro: Jim Anderson   Lessons: $35 / 30 Minutes
There is a Practice Putting Green, Chipping Green and a Driving
Range at Northstar. Bucket price: $3.00 They have a full restau-
rant and lounge open from 7:30 a.m. until 7 p.m. The Pro Shop
can fill all your golfing needs. Reservations can be made three
weeks in advance. Golf Cars are mandatory before 12:30 p.m.,
every day.   *The Golf Cars rent for $11.00 per person.

Facts & Figures:

Northstar-at-Tahoe Resort Golf Course is located in what used to
be a Basque sheep herding area in the early 1900's and remnants
of that era are still evident. Golfers are offered spectacular
mountain views as they traverse this forested course. The
fairways on the front 9 holes are generous, the back 9 are narrow
and lined by pine and aspen. Water hazards need to be dealt
with on 14 holes. Four sets of tees are offered, yardages range
6897 from the Gold to 5470 from the Red. Ratings and slopes
are: Gold 72/135, Blue 69.3/130, White 67.4/125 and Red 71.2/
134.

Old Brockway Golf Course

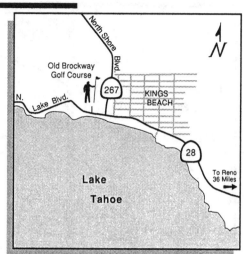

At Hwys. 267 & 28
Kings Beach, CA 96143

(916) 546-9909

9 Hole Course

Green Fees:

	Weekdays	Weekends
9 Holes:	$18 / $20*	$18 / $20*
18 Holes:	$26 / $30*	$26 / $30*
Twilight Rate:	$13.00	$15.00
Senior Discount: n.a.		

Outfitting:

Golf Cars - 9 Holes: $13.00   Golf Cars - 18 Holes: $20.00
     Pull Carts: $3.00   Clubs: $15.00

Lessons & More:

Club Pro: Dave Lewis   **Lessons:** $20 / $30
This course provides a Practice Putting Green, Chipping Green
and a Driving Range. Bucket price: $3.00. They have a full
restaurant open from 7 a.m. until 10 p.m. Their Pro Shop is
complete. Weekday reservations can be made up to one month
in advance, weekend reservations on the Monday prior. The
busiest day of the week is Saturday, least busy day is Wednes-
day. * Peak Season Fees

Facts & Figures:

This enchanting 9 hole course was built back in the 1920's. It
winds its way through the tall pines at the north end of Lake
Tahoe which can be seen often during play. The course is
considered to be of medium difficulty. It measures in length from
6474 yards from the White Tees to 5596 from the Red Tees if
played twice. Par is 70, slope 118/113. This course is comprised
of one par 5 hole, six par 4's and two par 3's.

Ponderosa Golf Course

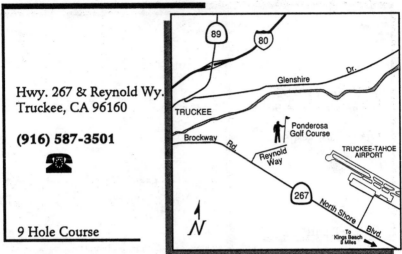

Hwy. 267 & Reynold Wy.
Truckee, CA 96160

(916) 587-3501

9 Hole Course

Green Fees:

	Weekdays	Weekends
9 Holes:	$20.00	$20.00
18 Holes:	$30.00	$30.00

Twilight Rate:
Senior Discount:

Outfitting:

Golf Cars - 9 Holes: $12.00	Golf Cars - 18 Holes: $20.00
Pull Carts: $2.00	Clubs: $10.00

Lessons & More:

Club Pro: Greg Carter   Lessons: $25 / 30 Minutes
Ponderosa provides a Practice Putting Green as their warm-up
facility. They have a Snack Bar serving hot dogs and light snacks
plus a variety of beverages. Their Pro Shop carries the golfers
basic necessities. Reservations can be made 10 days in advance.
Please call the Pro Shop for additional information on their green
fees. This course is open from the 1st of May to mid-October.

Facts & Figures:

The heavily forested terrain accounts for the course being called
Ponderosa. It is a varied 9 holes that both beginner and experienced golfers will enjoy, especially those who prefer to play a dry
course. Par here is 36 and it measures 3018 yards in length. It is
rated, with slopes, as follows: Blue 67.0/109, White 65.8/106 and
Red 68.2/108.

Rosewood Lakes Golf Course

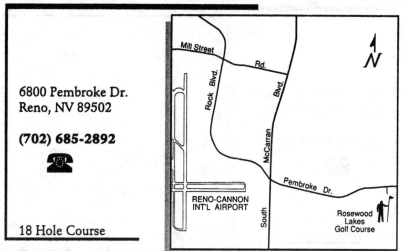

6800 Pembroke Dr.
Reno, NV 89502

(702) 685-2892

18 Hole Course

Green Fees:

	Weekdays	Weekends
9 Holes:	n.a.	n.a.
18 Holes:	$22.00	$22.00

Twilight Rate: $10.00
Senior Discount: n.a.

Outfitting:

Golf Cars - 9 Holes: $10.00	Golf Cars - 18 Holes: $16.00
Pull Carts: $3.00	Clubs: $15.00

Lessons & More:

Club Pro: Mike Mazzaferri   Lessons: $40 / 60 Minutes
Rosewood Lakes provides a Practice Putting Green, Chipping
Green and a Driving Range. They have a Snack Bar and a large
Pro Shop open for your convenience. Two teaching professionals
are available. Reservations are taken one week in advance. They
have Winter Rates that apply November 1st - April 1st. Washoe
County residents receive a discount on green fees.

Facts & Figures:

Rosewood Lakes Golf Course is the newest golf course in Reno.
It is a championship course which offers 4 sets of tees. From the
Gold Tees it will play for 6693 yards, 6104 from the Blue, 5481
from the White and 5082 from the Red. Ratings and slopes are:
71.1/127, 68.5/123, 65.8/119 and 64.1/115, respectively. The
course is very wide open, not a tree to be seen. There are water
hazards that can cause trouble. The course is built amid pro-
tected marshlands which prevent retrieving errant golf balls.

Sierra Sage Golf Course

6355 Silver Lake Road
Reno, NV 89506

(702) 972-1564

18 Hole Course

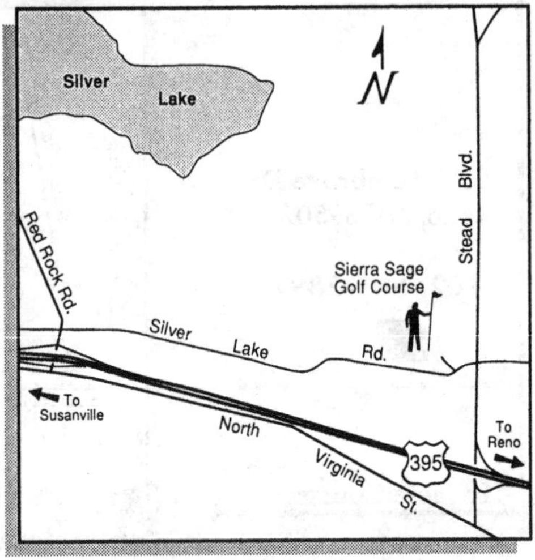

Green Fees:

	Weekdays	Weekends
9 Holes:	$9.00	$10.00
18 Holes:	*$13.00	*$15.00

Twilight Rate: n.a.
Senior Discount: Same as 9 Hole Rates to play 18 Holes

Outfitting:

Golf Cars - 9 Holes: $9.00   Golf Cars - 18 Holes: $18.00
Pull Carts: $2.00   Clubs: $12.00

Lessons & More:

Club Pro: Mike Mitchell   Lessons: $30 / Lesson
This course provides a Practice Putting Green, Chipping Green
and a Driving Range. Bucket price: $1.25 for 25 balls. They have
a Snack Bar open from 6 a.m. until 6 p.m. daily. The Pro Shop
can fill most of your golfing needs. Reservations can be made
one week in advance.   *Non-resident Green Fees for 18 Holes
is $18.00 Weekdays and $21.00 Weekends.

Facts & Figures:

This public 18 hole golf course began with only 9 holes and was
originally owned by the military. The county took it over in the
late 1960's, in 1973 another 9 holes were added. It is usually in
excellent shape from mid-May through October. The hills climb
gradually, the wide fairways surround four lakes. The course
measures 6623 yards from the Blue Tees, it is rated 68, slope 120.
From the White Tees it is 6207 yards long, slope 118 and from
the Red Tees it is 5573 yards long, rated 70.5, slope 113. Course
par is 71/72, course record is 63.

Tahoe-Reno
Area

176

Tahoe City Golf Course

251 North Lake Blvd.
Tahoe City, CA 95730

(916) 583-1516

9 Hole Course

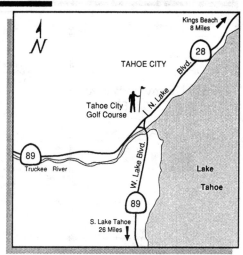

Green Fees:

	Weekdays	Weekends
9 Holes:	$20.00	$20.00
18 Holes:	$30.00	$30.00

Twilight Rate: $15.00
Senior Discount: With restrictions, $16.00 and $26.00

Outfitting:

Golf Cars - 9 Holes: $13.00   Golf Cars - 18 Holes: $20.00
     Pull Carts: $3.00   **Clubs:** $8.00 / $12.00

Lessons & More:

Club Pro: Don Hay   **Lessons:** $25 / Lesson
Tahoe City Golf Course offers a Practice Putting Green, Chipping
Green and a netted driving area. Bucket prices: $2.00 - $3.00.
Their restaurant serves from 6:30 a.m. until 6:00 p.m., but not
between 2:30 and 4:00. Their Pro Shop has a nice assortment of
golf equipment. Reservations can be made at anytime from April
to October.

Facts & Figures:

The condition of his 9 hole public course has recently been
upgraded. Back in 1917, when it was built by Queenie Dunn, the
greens were sand, now they are said to be some of the most
challenging on the lake. The golfer will play for 2583 yards from
the White Tees and 2402 from the Red. Par for the course is 33/
34. Eighteen hole ratings for the course are 63.4 from the White
Tees and 65.7 from the Red.

Tahoe Donner Golf Course

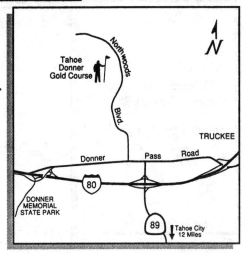

12850 Northwoods Blvd.
Truckee, CA 95737

(916) 587-9440

18 Hole Course

Green Fees:

	Weekdays	Weekends
9 Holes:	n.a.	n.a.
18 Holes:	$70.00	$70.00

Twilight Rate: $30.00
Senior Discount: n.a.

Outfitting:

Golf Cars - 9 Holes: $13.00	Golf Cars - 18 Holes: $26.00
Pull Carts: $4.00	Clubs: $18.00

Lessons & More:

Club Pro: Bruce A. Towle   **Lessons:** $40
This resort course offers a Practice Putting Green, Chipping Green and a Driving Range. Bucket price: $3.00 - $4.50. They have a full restaurant and snack bar open daily for your convenience. The Pro Shop carries a nice assortment of golf equipment. Reservations can be made two weeks in advance. Golf Cars included in Green Fees.

Facts & Figures:

Tahoe Donner is a resort course, surrounded by homes, that is open to public play. The fairways are tight, tree lined and hilly. The large greens allow for a variety of pin placements. The course is fairly long measuring 6963 yards from the Blue Tees, 6675 from the White Tees and 6031 from the Red Tees. Par for this course is 72/74. Course record is held by John Fought with a 66.

Tahoe Paradise Golf Course

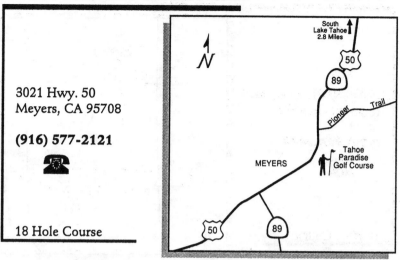

3021 Hwy. 50
Meyers, CA 95708

(916) 577-2121

18 Hole Course

Green Fees:

	Weekdays	Weekends
9 Holes:	$13.50	$13.50
18 Holes:	$21.00	$21.00
Twilight Rate:	$12.00	$12.00
Senior Discount: Yes		

Outfitting:

Golf Cars - 9 Holes: $11.00   Golf Cars - 18 Holes: $17.00
Pull Carts: Clubs: $5.00 - $7.50

Lessons & More:

Club Pro: David Beeman   Lessons: Yes
Tahoe Paradise Golf Course provides a Putting Green and a
Driving Range. They have a Snack Bar open for your conve-
nience and a small Pro Shop. Reservations are taken at anytime.
Please check with the Pro Shop for a possible increase in Green
Fees.

Facts & Figures:

Tahoe Paradise Golf Course is an executive 18 hole course in the
scenic mountains four miles from Lake Tahoe. Accuracy plays a
major role is you wish to score well, the fairways are narrow and
not at all forgiving. From the Men's Tees the course is 4070
yards long, par is 66 and from the Women's Tees it is 3886 yards
long with a par of 69.

Tahoe-Reno
Area

Washoe County Golf Course

2601 S. Arlington Ave.
Reno, NV 89505

(702) 785-4286

18 Hole Course

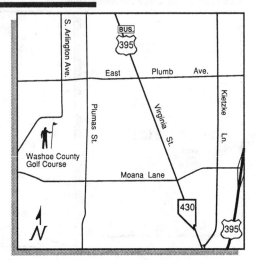

Green Fees:

	Weekdays	Weekends
9 Holes:	$9.00	$10.00
18 Holes:	$13.00	* $15.00

Twilight Rate: $10.00
Senior Discount: $8.00 for 9 Holes, $10.00 for 18 Holes

Outfitting:

Golf Cars - 9 Holes: $9.00   Golf Cars - 18 Holes: $18.00
Pull Carts: $2.00   Clubs: $15.00

Lessons & More:

Club Pro: Brett Torvtnen   **Lessons:** $40 / 60 Minutes
Washoe County Golf Course provides a Practice Putting Green,
Chipping Green and a Driving Range. Bucket prices: $2.00 -
$4.00. Their Restaurant is open daily from 6 a.m. until 6 p.m.
The Pro Shop can help fill most of your golfing needs. Reservations can be made one week in advance. * Green Fees of $15.00
entitles you to all day play, non-resident fee is $21.00

Tahoe-Reno
Area

Facts & Figures:

Washoe County Golf Course opened in 1934 and is Reno's
oldest. This well established course sits right in the middle of
town. You play a flat front 9 and a hilly back 9. The greens are
small, the fairways are of medium width. There are three lakes
and a ditch that runs through the entire course. It plays for a total
of 6695 yards and has a par of 72, rated 70 with a slope of 119.
From the Red Tees it is 5973 yards long and has a par of 74, rated
72.4 and slope 120. The course record is held by Ben Hogan
with a 63.

Wildcreek Golf Course

3500 Sullivan Lane
Sparks, NV 89431

(702) 673-3100

27 Hole Course

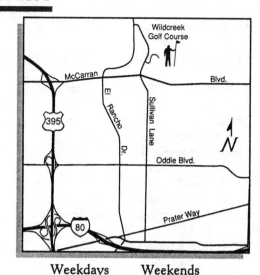

Green Fees:

	Weekdays	Weekends
9 Holes:	$20.00	$20.00
18 Holes:	$37.00	$37.00

Twilight Rate: $22.00 with Golf Car
Senior Discount: n.a.

Outfitting:

Golf Cars - 9 Holes: Golf Cars - 18 Holes: Included
   Pull Carts: $1.00   Clubs: $18 / $20

Lessons & More:

Club Pro: Fred Elliott   Lessons: $40 / Lesson
This course provides a Practice Putting Green, Chipping Green
and a Driving Range. Bucket price: $2.50 - $3.00 They have a
Snack Bar and a lounge open for your convenience. The Pro
Shop carries an extensive golf inventory. Reservations can be
made seven days in advance. **Executive 9 Hole Course Green
Fees are $8.00 for 9 Holes and $10.00 for 18 Holes. Golf Cars
included in Green Fees for 18 Hole Course only.**

Facts & Figures:

Wildcreek Golf Course consists of a championship 18 hole course
and an executive 9. The 9 hole course is 1400 yards long, par 27.
Holes range from 100 to 220 yards in length. The 18 hole course
will play for 6932 yards from the Championship tees and 5472
from the forward tees, par is 72. This is a nice rolling course
enhanced by 6 lakes and a creek that often comes into play. The
greens are sloping and fast. Wildcreek has been open for play
since 1979 and has played host to 3 senior tour events.

Tahoe-Reno Area

181

Course Name	City	Size	Page
Adobe Creek GC (707) 765-3000	Petaluma	18 Holes	p. 144
Aetna Springs GC (707) 965-2115	Pope Valley	9 Holes	p. 59
Ancil Hoffman GC (916) 482-5660	Carmichael	18 Holes	p. 68
Aptos Par 3 (408) 688-5000	Aptos	9 Holes	p. 130
Aptos Seascape GC (408) 688-3213	Aptos	18 Holes	p. 131
Bay Meadows GC (415) 341-7204	San Mateo	9 Holes	p. 101
Bennett Valley GC (707) 528-3673	Santa Rosa	18 Holes	p. 145
Bijou Golf Course (916) 544-5500	So. Lake Tahoe	9 Holes	p. 161
Bing Maloney GC (916) 428-9401	Sacramento	18 Holes	p. 69
Blackberry Farm GC (408) 253-9200	Cupertino	9 Holes	p. 110
Blue Rock Spgs. Muni. (707) 643-8476	Vallejo	18 Holes	p. 139
Bodega Harbour GL (707) 875-3538	Bodega Bay	18 Holes	p. 146
Bolado Park GC (408) 628-9995	Tres Pinos	9 Holes	p. 84
Boulder Creek G & CC (408) 338-2111	Boulder Creek	18 Holes	p. 132
Boundary Oak GC (510) 934-6211	Walnut Creek	18 Holes	p. 26
Brookside Muni. GC (702) 322-6009	Reno	9 Holes	p. 162
Buchanan Field GC (510) 682-1846	Concord	9 Holes	p. 27
Campus Commons GC (916) 922-5861	Sacramento	9 Holes	p. 70
Canyon Lakes GC (510) 735-6511	San Ramon	18 Holes	p. 28
Carson Valley GC (702) 265-3181	Gardnerville	18 Holes	p. 163
Casserly Par 3 GC (408) 724-1654	Watsonville	9 Holes	p. 133
Chardonnay Club (707) 257-8950	Napa	18 Holes	p. 60

Course Name	City	Size	Page
Cherry Island GC (916) 911-0770	Elverta	18 Holes	p. 71
Chimney Rock GC (707) 255-3363	Napa	9 Holes	p. 61
Cordova Golf Course (916) 362-1196	Sacramento	18 Holes	p. 72
Crystal Spgs. Golf Club (415) 342-0603	Burlingame	18 Holes	p. 102
Cypress Golf Course (415) 992-5155	Colma	9 Holes	p. 103
Cypress Greens GC (408) 238-3485	San Jose	18 Holes	p. 116
Davis Muni. GC (916) 756-4010	Davis	18 Holes	p. 73
Dayton Valley CC (702) 246-7888	Dayton	18 Holes	p. 164
De Laveaga GC (408) 423-7212	Santa Cruz	18 Holes	p. 134
Deep Cliff GC (408) 253-5357	Cupertino	18 Holes	p. 111
Del Monte GC (408) 373-2436	Monterey	18 Holes	p. 46
Diablo Creek GC (510) 686-6262	Concord	18 Holes	p. 29
Diablo Hills GC (510) 939-7372	Walnut Creek	9 Holes	p. 30
Diamond Oaks GC (916) 783-4947	Roseville	18 Holes	p. 74
Dry Creek Ranch GC (209) 745-2330	Galt	18 Holes	p. 75
Eagle Valley GC (702) 887-2380	Carson City	36 Holes	p. 165
Earl Fry Golf Course (510) 522-4321	Alameda	18 Holes	p. 10
Edgewood Tahoe GC (702) 588-3566	Lake Tahoe	18 Holes	p. 166
El Dorado Hills GC (916) 933-6552	El Dorado Hills	18 Holes	p. 76
Emerald Hills GC (415) 368-7820	Redwood City	9 Holes	p. 104
Escalon Golf Course (209) 838-1277	Escalon	9 Holes	p. 94
Fairgrounds Golf Course (707) 546-2469	Santa Rosa	9 Holes	p. 147

Course Name	City	Size	Page
Fleming Golf Course (415) 661-1865	San Francisco	9 Holes	p. 87
Foothill Golf Center (916) 725-3355	Sacramento	9 Holes	p. 77
Forest Lake GC (209) 369-5451	Acampo	18 Holes	p. 95
Fountaingrove Resort (707) 579-4653	Santa Rosa	18 Holes	p. 148
Franklin Canyon GC (510) 799-6191	Rodeo	18 Holes	p. 31
Galbraith Golf Course (510) 569-9411	Oakland	18 Holes	p. 11
Gavilan Golf Course (408) 848-1363	Gilroy	9 Holes	p. 112
Gilroy Golf Course (408) 842-2501	Gilroy	9 Holes	p. 113
Glenbrook GC (702) 749-5201	Glenbrook	9 Holes	p. 167
Gleneagles Int'l. GC (415) 587-2425	San Francisco	9 Holes	p. 88
Golden Gate Park GC (415) 751-8987	San Francisco	9 Holes	p. 89
Green Tree GC (707) 448-1420	Vacaville	27 Holes	p. 140
Haggin Oaks GC (916) 481-4507	Sacramento	36 Holes	p. 78
Half Moon Bay GL (415) 726-4438	Half Moon Bay	18 Holes	p. 105
Harding Park GC (415) 664-4690	San Francisco	18 Holes	p. 90
Hidden Valley Lake (707) 987-3035	Middletown	18 Holes	p. 62
Hill Country GC (408) 779-4136	Morgan Hill	18 Holes	p. 114
Incline Village Resort (702) 832-1144 - Championship (702) 832-1150 - Executive	Incline Village	36 Holes	p. 168
Indian Valley GC (415) 897-1118	Novato	18 Holes	p. 40
Jack Clark GC (510) 522-4321	Alameda	18 Holes	p. 12
King City GC (408) 385-4546	King City	9 Holes	p. 47

Course Name	City	Size	Page
La Contenta Golf Club (209) 772-1081	Valley Springs	18 Holes	p. 96
Laguna Seca Golf Club (408) 373-3701	Monterey	18 Holes	p. 48
Lake Chabot Muni. (510) 351-5812	Oakland	18 Holes	p. 13
Lake Ridge GC (702) 825-2200	Reno	18 Holes	p. 169
Lake Tahoe GC (916) 577-0788	So. Lake Tahoe	18 Holes	p. 170
Las Positas GC (510) 443-3122	Livermore	27 Holes	p. 14
Lighthouse G&CC (916) 372-4949	West Sacramento	18 Holes	p. 79
Lincoln Park GC (415) 221-9911	San Francisco	18 Holes	p. 91
Lone Tree GC (510) 757-5200	Antioch	18 Holes	p. 32
Los Arroyos GC (707) 938-8835	Sonoma	9 Holes	p. 149
Manteca Park GC (209) 825-2500	Manteca	18 Holes	p. 97
Marina GC (510) 895-2164	San Leandro	9 Holes	p. 15
Mill Valley GC (415) 388-9982	Mill Valley	9 Holes	p. 41
Mount St. Helena GC (707) 942-9966	Calistoga	9 Holes	p. 63
Mountain Shadows GC (707) 584-7766	Rohnert Park	36 Holes	p. 150
Napa Muni. GC (707) 255-4333	Napa	18 Holes	p. 64
Northgate Golf Club (702) 747-7577	Reno	18 Holes	p. 171
Northstar-at-Tahoe (916) 587-0290	Truckee	18 Holes	p. 172
Northwood GC (707) 865-1116	Monte Rio	9 Holes	p. 151
Oakhurst Country Club (510) 672-9737	Clayton	18 Holes	p. 33
Oakmont Golf Club (707) 538-2454 - East (707) 539-0414 - West	Santa Rosa	36 Holes	p. 152

Course
Index

Course Name	City	Size	Page
Old Brockway GC (916) 546-9909	Kings Beach	9 Holes	p. 173
Pacific Grove Muni. GC (408) 648-3177	Pacific Grove	18 Holes	p. 49
Pajaro Valley Golf Club (408) 724-3851	Watsonville	18 Holes	p. 50
Palo Alto Muni. GC (415) 856-0881	Palo Alto	18 Holes	p. 115
Parkway Golf Course (510) 656-6862	Fremont	9 Holes	p. 16
Pasatiempo Golf Club (408) 459-9155	Santa Cruz	18 Holes	p. 135
Peacock Gap G&CC (415) 453-4940	San Rafael	18 Holes	p. 42
Pebble Beach Golf Links (408) 624-6611	Pebble Beach	18 Holes	p. 51
Pine Meadow Public GC (510) 288-2881	Martinez	9 Holes	p. 34
Pittsburg Golf &CC (510) 427-4940	Pittsburg	18 Holes	p. 35
Pleasant Hills G&CC (408) 238-3485	San Jose	18 Holes	p. 116
Pleasanton Fairways GC (510) 462-4653	Pleasanton	9 Holes	p. 17
Ponderosa GC (916) 587-3501	Truckee	9 Holes	p. 174
Poppy Hills GC (408) 625-2035	Pebble Beach	18 Holes	p. 52
Pruneridge Golf Club (408) 248-4424	Santa Clara	9 Holes	p. 117
Rancho Cañada GC (408) 624-0111	Carmel	36 Holes	p. 53
Rancho Solano (707) 429-4653	Fairfield	18 Holes	p. 141
Ridgemark Golf & CC (408) 637-1010	Hollister	36 Holes	p. 85
Riverside GC (408) 463-0622	Coyote	18 Holes	p. 118
Roseville Rolling Greens (619) 797-9986	Roseville	9 Holes	p. 80
Rosewood Lakes GC (702) 685-2892	Reno	18 Holes	p. 175

Course Name	City	Size	Page
Salinas Fairway GC (408) 758-7300	Salinas	18 Holes	p. 54
San Geronimo GC (415) 488-4030	San Geronimo	18 Holes	p. 43
San Jose Muni. GC (408) 441-4653	San Jose	18 Holes	p. 119
San Mateo Muni. GC (415) 347-1461	San Mateo	18 Holes	p. 106
San Ramon Royal Vista (510) 828-6100	San Ramon	18 Holes	p. 36
Santa Clara G&TC (408) 980-9515	Santa Clara	18 Holes	p. 120
Santa Teresa Golf Club (408) 225-2650	San Jose	18 Holes	p. 121
Sea Ranch Golf Links (707) 785-2467	Sea Ranch	9 Holes	p. 153
Sebastopol GC (707) 823-9852	Sebastopol	9 Holes	p. 154
Sharp Park GC (415) 359-3380	Pacifica	18 Holes	p. 107
Sherwood Greens GC (408) 758-7333	Salinas	9 Holes	p. 55
Shoreline Golf Links (415) 969-2041	Mountain View	18 Holes	p. 122
Sierra Sage GC (702) 972-1564	Reno	18 Holes	p. 176
Skywest GC (510) 278-6188	Hayward	18 Holes	p. 18
Sonoma Golf Club (707) 996-0300	Sonoma	18 Holes	p. 155
Spring Hills GC (408) 724-1404	Watsonville	18 Holes	p. 136
Spring Valley GC (408) 262-1722	Milpitas	18 Holes	p. 123
Springtown Muni. GC (510) 455-5695	Livermore	9 Holes	p. 19
Spyglass Hill GC (408) 624-3811	Pebble Beach	18 Holes	p. 56
Summit Pointe Golf Club (408) 262-8813	Milpitas	18 Holes	p. 124
Sunken Gardens Muni. (408) 739-6588	Sunnyvale	9 Holes	p. 125

Course Name	City	Size	Page
Sunnyvale Muni. GC (408) 738-3666	Sunnyvale	18 Holes	p. 126
Sunol Valley Golf Club (510) 862-0414	Sunol	36 Holes	p. 20
Swenson Park GC (209) 477-0774	Stockton	27 Holes	p. 98
Tahoe City GC (916) 583-1516	Tahoe City	9 Holes	p. 177
Tahoe Donner GC (916) 587-9440	Truckee	18 Holes	p. 178
Tahoe Paradise GC (916) 577-2121	Meyers	18 Holes	p. 179
Tayman Park GC (707) 433-4275	Healdsburg	9 Holes	p. 156
The Island GC (510) 684-2654	Bethel Island	18 Holes	p. 37
The Links at Spanish Bay (408) 624-6611	Pebble Beach	18 Holes	p. 57
Thunderbird GC (408) 259-3355	San Jose	18 Holes	p. 127
Tilden Park GC (510) 848-7373	Berkeley	18 Holes	p. 38
Tony Lema GC (510) 895-2162	San Leandro	18 Holes	p. 21
Valley Gardens GC (408) 438-3058	Scotts Valley	9 Holes	p. 137
Van Buskirk Park GC (209) 464-5629	Stockton	18 Holes	p. 99
Washoe County GC (702) 785-4286	Reno	18 Holes	p. 180
Wikiup GC (707) 546-8787	Santa Rosa	9 Holes	p. 157
Wildcreek GC (702) 673-3100	Sparks	27 Holes	p. 181
William Land Park GC (916) 455-5014	Sacramento	9 Holes	p. 81
Willow Park GC (510) 537-8989	Castro Valley	18 Holes	p. 22
Windsor Golf Club (707) 838-7888	Windsor	18 Holes	p. 158

Course Index

PRIVATE COURSES

Alameda County
Castlewood Country Club	Pleasanton	(415) 846-5151
Claremont Country Club	Oakland	(415) 655-2431
Sequoyah Country Club	Oakland	(415) 632-4069

Contra Costa County
Blackhawk Country Club	Danville	(415) 820-1118
Contra Costa Country Club	Pleasant Hill	(415) 685-8288
Crow Canyon Country Club	Danville	(415) 866-8300
Diablo Country Club	Diablo	(415) 837-9233
Discovery Bay Country Club	Discovery Bay	(415) 634-0700
Mira Vista Country Club	El Cerrito	(415) 237-7045
Moraga Country Club	Moraga	(415) 376-2253
Orinda Country Club	Orinda	(415) 254-0811
Richmond Country Club	Richmond	(415) 232-7815
Rossmoor Golf Course	Walnut Creek	(415) 933-2607
Round Hill G & CC	Alamo	(415) 837-7424

Marin County
Marin Country Club	Novato	(415) 479-0252
Meadow Country Club	Fairfax	(415) 456-9393

Monterey County
Carmel Valley G & CC	Carmel Valley	(408) 624-2779
Carmel Valley Ranch	Carmel	(408) 626-2511
Corral de Tierra Country Club	Salinas	(408) 484-1325
Cypress Point Club	Pebble Beach	(408) 624-2223
Fort Ord Golf Course	Fort Ord	(408) 899-0636
Monterey Peninsula CC	Pebble Beach	(408) 372-8141
Salinas G & CC	Salinas	(408) 449-1526
U.S. Navy Golf Course	Monterey	(408) 646-2167

PRIVATE COURSES

Napa County
Meadowood Resort Hotel	St. Helena	(707) 963-3646
Napa Valley Country Club	Napa	(707) 252-1114
Silverado Country Club	Napa	(707) 257-5460

Sacramento County
Del Paso Country Club	Sacramento	(916) 489-3681
Lawrence Links Golf Course	Sacramento	(916) 643-3313
Mather AFB Golf Course	Sacramento	(916) 364-3731
North Ridge Country Club	Fair Oaks	(916) 967-5716
Rancho Murieta County Club	Rancho Murieta	(916) 985-7200
Sunrise Golf Course	Citrus Heights	(916) 723-8854
Valley Hi Country Club	Elk Grove	(916) 423-2170

San Francisco County
Olympic Country Club	San Francisco	(415) 587-8338
Presidio Army Golf Course	Presidio	(415) 751-1322
San Francisco Golf Club	San Francisco	(415) 469-4122

San Joaquin County
Elkhorn Country Club	Stockton	(209) 477-0252
Spring Creek G & CC	Ripon	(209) 599-3630
Stockton G & CC	Stockton	(209) 466-6221
Tracy G & CC	Stockton	(209) 835-9463
Woodbridge G & CC	Woodbridge	(209) 369-2371

PRIVATE COURSES

San Mateo County

Burlingame Country Club	Hillsborough	(415) 342-0750
California Golf Club	S. San Francisco	(415) 589-0144
Green Hills Country Club	Milbrae	(415) 583-0882
Lake Merced G & CC	Daly City	(415) 755-2239
Menlo Country Club	Woodside	(415) 366-9910
Moffett Field Golf Course	NAS Moffett Field	(415) 966-5332
Peninsula G & CC	San Mateo	(415) 345-9521
Sharon Heights G & CC	Menlo Park	(415) 854-6429

Santa Clara County

Almaden G & CC	San Jose	(408) 268-4653
La Rinconada Country Club	Los Gatos	(408) 395-4220
Los Altos G & CC	Los Altos	(415) 948-2146
Palo Alto Hills Country Club	Palto Alto	(415) 948-2320
San Jose Country Club	San Jose	(408) 258-3636
Saratoga Country Club	Saratoga	(408) 253-5494
Stanford Golf Course	Stanford	(415) 323-0944
The Villages G & CC	San Jose	(408) 274-3220

Solano County

Green Valley Country Club	Suisun City	(707) 864-0473

Sonoma County

Petaluma G & CC	Petaluma	(707) 762-7041
Santa Rosa G & CC	Santa Rosa	(707) 564-6617